'Within just 30 days Phillips' methods will have you living and working more efficiently, allowing you extra time to do more of the things that make you a happy and better person.'
Eddie Barrett Ph.D., Vice President of Sales & Account Management,
Intellinex LLC – the Learning Venture of Ernst & Young LLP

'I really did find the book to be useful, and I'll recommend it to our delegates on the "Working Smarter" and "Planning And Organizing" workshops which I facilitate here at Virgin Atlantic.'
Geoff Penn, Learning & Development Cons&t&nt Vi.&&antic Airways

'Simon leaves no stone n&&&&, you beco&&&more &ttective. Read&& book twice, once to be inspired and the&&&&&&&owing&&&oach&&to double your&&&uveness.'
Nicola Carew, Director&&&&&&&h, &&&

'Modern communications&&&he&&stinction between wor&& and home so th&&e is even more need to manage our m&&&&&luable resour&&&&in o&&&&o achieve a sensible work-life balance. In this book, Simon&&&&&&sho&&us how to do it.'
Lynette Swift, Managing Dire&&&&&&Wor&&&&&&&-Li&&&&&&&&&&ecialists)

'Simon has served up a dish of real content and "personality". Having absorbed the key messages I have two clear Goals – to use this book to manage not just my work life but life as a whole; and secondly, to make this compulsory reading for my senior management team.'
Mark Miller, Managing Director, Portfolio Catering

'Simon is a person of great passion and total commitment and this shines out of every page in the book – read it or weep!'
Alisdair Wiseman – Managing Director – The Innovation Zone

'Real advice and tips you can easily use straight away to increase your effectiveness and time management. So now I can play more golf – fantastic!'
Martin Hopley, Managing Director, Golfalot.com

'Powerful ideas, clearly explained – if you are too busy to read this book, get up early one morning and read it anyway, it will give you new ideas on how to get more of the most precious commodity in the world – some more time.'
Malcom Follos, Bowman Group

'This is much more than a thought provoking good read but a guide to action. I heartedly recommend it to anyone who wants to make a real difference to their lives.'
Gerry McAuley, Managing Director, Themeus Consulting & Training

'Knowledge Workers, remote or virtual teams, portfolio managers – they all need the tools and behaviours described in this book. I will be recommending it to all our clients. An invaluable read and a powerful guide for the information age.'
Andrew Kinnear, Director, OfficeontheWeb

'There is only one person who can give you work life balance and that is you – this book shows how it is possible for everyone to achieve it.'
Rachel Robbins, HR Manager, Wirral Social Services

TIME
MANAGEMENT

24/7

How to **<u>double</u>** your effectiveness

SIMON PHILLIPS

London · Burr Ridge IL · New York · St Louis · San Francisco · Auckland · Bogotá ·
Caracas · Lisbon · Madrid · Mexico · Milan · Montreal · New Delhi · Panama ·
Paris · San Juan · São Paulo · Singapore · Sydney · Tokyo · Toronto

Time Management 24/7: How to Double Your Effectiveness
Simon Phillips
007709963X

Published by McGraw-Hill Professional
Shoppenhangers Road
Maidenhead
Berkshire
SL6 2QL
Telephone: 44 (0) 1628 502 500
Fax: 44 (0) 1628 770 224
Website: www.mcgraw-hill.co.uk

British Library Cataloguing in Publication Data
A catalogue record for this book is available from the British Library

Library of Congress Cataloging in Publication Data
The library of Congress data for this book
is available from the Library of Congress

Sponsoring Editor: Elizabeth Robinson
Editorial Assistant: Sarah Butler
Business Marketing Manager: Elizabeth McKeever
Senior Production Manager: Max Elvey
Production Editor: Eleanor Hayes

Produced for McGraw-Hill by
RefineCatch Limited, Bungay, Suffolk
Text design by Gray Publishing Ltd
Printed and bound in the UK by Clays Ltd
Cover design by Simon Levy Associates

McGraw-Hill books are available at special quantity discounts. Please contact the
Corporate Sales Executive at the above address.

To follow up on any of the information in this book, seminar schedules, coaching or
corporate speaking inquiries please contact Simon Phillips at Simesco Limited, Liberty Suite,
261 Dedworth Road, Windsor, SL4 4JS. Tel: (+44) 1753 623793
Email: simes@simonphillips.biz – or visit us at www.simonphillips.biz

To my parents – Brenda and John – for teaching me the meaning of the word Love.

Contents

Contents

Acknowledgements

I thought that this would be the most difficult part of the book to write – I couldn't possibly include everyone that I would wish to acknowledge. Then I sat back and began to think through the evolution of this book and everything became crystal clear.

To start, my folks had the foresight to have another child after parenting two enterprising lads already (Ian and Stuart). Then, at the age of 10, I met Ray Lewis, who not only taught me with immense skill and humour but was also the first person to inject me with a belief that anything was possible. Moving on, friends like David Hellyar, Richard James and Neil Sparnon kept me level-headed through my teens – this particular trio did their best to steer me way off track! Then there is John Garland, the man who introduced me to claret, Mozart and a love of history that will always remain in my heart.

Friendship is a critical ingredient for life, and I am privileged to count as friends Alan Sykes, Hoppers and Carol, Dr and Mrs Finlay, Angus and Tereasa, Flash, Sarah and Rob, Julian and Deborah, Katherine and Mark, Gordon and Andrea, Christina, Sarah and Simon, Sam, Emma, Ady, Mark, Carol and, of course, Darren, Mandi and Donna. Not forgetting Andrew, Chris P-B, Chris W, Eddie, Gerry, Gordon, Iain, Jillian, Leslie, Nicola, Pat and, of course, Rahul. These days, when I am not travelling around the UK visiting such friends, I am blessed with a wonderful family that covers most of Wales, extends from Plymouth to Poole and ventures into London – it's a good job I love driving!

Then my mentors: first, Jerry De Groot, tutor extraordinaire, matchmaker supreme and the man who encouraged me to write, so if you don't like this book, he's the man to blame (if you do like it, please write directly to me); secondly, Damon Lawrenson, motivator, entrepreneur, fellow dreamer and trusted friend.

Finally, my wonderful wife Clare and our first little miracle – Adam Powell Phillips – for inspiring my dreams and making me feel like the luckiest man alive.

Foreword

In his recent best seller, *Business @ The Speed of Thought*, Bill Gates asserts, 'Business is going to change more in the next ten years than it has in the last fifty'. Few of us would disagree with this trend in corporate life.

This is a book that provides an insight into the flexible, adaptable and, most important of all, specific individual strategies that can be used to manage the increasingly scarce resource of 'time'.

Two years ago when I first encountered Simon Phillips I was managing one of the largest blue chip training operations in the country, with over 200 managers and trainers spread geographically from Aberdeen to Exeter, and from Newport to Peterborough.

My team and I faced major challenges in coordinating an operation of this size that was delivering around 200,000 delegate days of training every year, while at the same time having the goal of rationalizing the overall function by about 50% over an eighteen month period. When faced with such demands one of the key requirements to achieving success is the effective use of time.

Back in 2000 all my managers and I employed some form of time management system. However, as so often happens our systems had all, to some degree, fallen into disuse. The great thing about the *Time Management 24/7* system is the recognition that the world in which we now operate requires not only new time management strategies, but also new methodologies and systems, systems that fully utilise the technology that is now available.

Simon Phillips's programme allowed my management team and I to harness technology as an enabler rather than a constraint to effective time management. We embraced the system and it was certainly a positive factor in helping us to achieve both business and personal goals.

As you read this book it will become apparent how essential it is in this day and age to employ a time management system that can keep pace with the speed of change.

Simon Phillips brings a fresh and radical approach to the practice of time management, moving the concept very much into the business world of today. This book should become an essential tool for any time challenged individual. Let's face it that's all of us.

Ron Oliver, MBA, BEd, MCIPD
Former Head of the University for Lloyds TSB

Introduction – everything changes but some things stay the same

One of the most important skills you can possess in today's 24/7 world is time management; but don't take my word for it. In a survey of the most desirable traits of a good 'teleworker', conducted recently by the UK's former Department for Employment and Education (DfEE), time management was one of the top six skills identified. Similarly, a study of the impact of electronic communication on organizations concluded that a 'Millennium Worker' would not succeed without good time management.[1] It seems that consensus is starting to form around the idea that time management is a skill that is central not only to success but also to survival.

However, for many years time management has not been fashionable. It has typically been at the bottom of the list of training priorities for many companies and individuals, with courses on how to use new technology, the Internet and new telecommunication tools at the top of the list instead. As a result, many people have assumed that just having access to new technology – such as handheld organizers and desktop calendars – is sufficient for them to place a tick in the box alongside time management. Sadly, this is not the case, because none of the new tools can replace the fundamental principles of effective time management. Indeed, if left unchecked, these new tools can make the process of working in teams even more difficult, and the task of organizing yourself a miserable experience.

This book takes a fresh look at time management in order to re-establish it as a core skill – for if you can get the basics of time management right, success in every area of your life can be achieved more smoothly.

---

[1] 'Nil By Mouth', a joint report by Andersen Consulting (now Accenture) and Investors In People.

It is with 'You' that we start. In preparing this book, I have thought more about the 'why' of time management than the 'how'. There is a comprehensive range of tips and techniques to help you throughout the book, but all of these are just tinkering if you don't tackle the fundamental questions of 'who you are' (Chapter 1) and 'why you want to be a better time manager' (Chapter 2). To help you get to this point I will walk you through the creation of your Life Map, constructed from the four key areas of life – Live, Love, Learn and Leave a Legacy. From here, we will break things down even further and look at your goals – how to set them and, more importantly, how to keep them on track and achieve them. Then, in 'An introduction to Time Styles', I will show you how to understand your own approach to time management and also a quick way to tune in to the approaches of others to the everyday time management challenges that face us all.

The next chapter, 'Manage yourself', is a direct response to some of the key issues that face people working from home – or away from traditional concepts of the workplace, at least. Interestingly, most of the challenges – daily habits, prioritizing and procrastination – are not new. What are new are some of the techniques for overcoming these challenges and a dynamic tool that will really double your effectiveness – the Results Cyclone. Chapter 6, on the other hand, is about managing others, especially the most difficult person on everyone's list – the boss! Discover how being able to differentiate between a Bull, an Ostrich and a Warrior could save you hours, if not days, during your lifetime. Finally, learn why saying 'No' is sometimes the best thing that you can do for others and how, by asking good questions, you can also be the most helpful person they know.

While the first half of the book reassesses the standard topics of traditional time management, the second half looks at some of the new approaches (Chapter 7), tools (Chapter 8) and principles (Chapter 9) that are revolutionizing the world of personal effectiveness. In essence, this section is a review of the 'how', 'what' and 'why' of the most effective methods for maximizing your performance, and the performance of your teams, in the 21st century.

'Managing life @ digital speed' looks at proven strategies for tackling the most challenging components of modern working – email, e-meetings, mobile phones, voicemail and knowledge sharing – while 'Advanced digital time-ology' looks at just some of the ways existing technology is being used to push the boundaries of effective time management.

By the time you get to the 'Close' of this book, I hope that you will be inspired to emulate some of the behaviours of our digital entrepreneur or, at the very least, recognize that 'doubling your effectiveness' is **not** about helping you get better at managing your time so that you can 'fit more in'. Our mission at Simesco has always been to help people achieve a better balance in their lives. If you apply the ideas, techniques and principles in this book, you will certainly be able to **do** more. Your challenge is to go beyond this and **be** a more effective person – in all the areas of your life that you choose.

❝ There is nothing so useless as doing efficiently that which should not be done at all. ❞

Peter Drucker

1   This is your life – take responsibility

Have you ever said that there never seems to be enough time to do all the things that you have to do, not to mention the things that you would like to do? Well, a recent subject of the television programme *This Is Your Life* managed all of the following:

a. world pentathlon champion

b. Olympic pentathlon champion

c. British and European pentathlon champion

d. Israeli Ambulance Service volunteer

e. charity worker for Merlin (a UK-based charity which provides health care for people caught up in crises and disasters around the world)

f. Cambridge University graduate

g. qualified medical doctor

. . . by the age of 29!

The subject was Stephanie Cook, and I think her story is a great reminder that it is possible to do an incredible amount with the limited time we have at our disposal. Sometimes it is very easy to get wrapped up in how busy we are – but we are all given exactly the same amount of time to play with, so why is it that some people seem to get so much more done than others? I would suggest it is for just one all-encompassing reason:

    ❛ Successful people use their time effectively. ❜

When you use your time effectively you can achieve everything of which you are capable. Or, to paraphrase my mentor, good time management allows you to 'be the best you you can be'. It is no accident that enlightened organizations are again beginning to invest in good time management courses as the foundation stones upon which they can build effective individuals, teams and leaders.

Good time management is a catalyst. The best thing about time management, though, is that you don't need any other skills to get started. Getting started requires only that you bring yourself along and that you commit to accepting responsibility for your life. Later in this chapter we will look at one of the key assets of every successful time manager – the ability to accept responsibility. I will show you how it helps you to focus on the main issue – moving forward. Before that, let's discover who you are.

Who are you?

To make progress in any area of life, it is essential to recognize that life is not a spectator sport and that no one is more intent on helping you get past the winning post (however you define it) than the person sitting in your seat. The best way to fulfil your own potential is just to be yourself. You will not achieve great results from this book, or any other personal development book, if you are only imitating someone else.

In Memory of . . .

I know that it's sad to contemplate this, but how would you like to be remembered when you die? What contribution to the world, and to those around you, will outlive your physical being? While a lot of people die and become a statistic and many more are forgotten altogether, there are some people who continue to be remembered by name as a direct result of their contribution to the lives of others. How will you be remembered? As a devoted partner, a beloved parent, a committed philanthropist, a courageous leader, a selfless pillar of the community, a dedicated teacher, an inspiring coach?

ACTIVITIES

1. Why not write your epitaph today? Think about the most important people in your life and what you hope to have left in their hearts. Focus on the way you will have behaved rather than on the actual things you will have done.

2. Write a list of the five most important things/people in your life right now.

   It is said that you can tell how much importance an individual places on something or someone by the amount of time they spend doing it or being with them. If the list you have just created is not representative of where you are spending your time, move on to the next activity.

3. Commit to making the items/people on your list that you are currently neglecting a focus for the beneficial results you achieve from implementing the other activities in this book.

Discovering You

There is an ancient saying, attributed to many different civilizations, that suggests that in order to understand another person, you should walk a mile in their shoes. Adapting this saying for our purposes here, I would contend that to understand yourself fully, you should walk the same distance in your own shoes. This is not as mad as it sounds. How often do we take time out to reflect on our lives: what we are contributing, how we benefit those around us, who we have become? The rest of this book will take you on that journey, but for now I want you to make the following commitment:

‘ I will take every opportunity to be more self-conscious for a week. ’

To do this, you will need to do some of the following:

- Listen to how people talk to you.
- Listen to how you talk to others.
- Reflect on the number of times you get annoyed or frustrated.
- Check how many times you smile.

7

- Monitor how many times you say 'thank you' genuinely.
- Check how often you plan, implement and review your actions.
- Reflect on how many new friends you have made.

So, what's the point? Well, until you know what defines you, how can you be yourself? Until you know who you are, how can you hope to know what you want out of life and what you can contribute to the lives of others? Some people we have consulted on this suggest that they 'just know', and to a large extent this is true. However, it is at times of pressure, when things are not going to plan, that we tend to adopt behaviours that are atypical. In these moments, a better self-understanding can help you to monitor your behaviour and express the real you.

I overheard a conversation recently that reminded me of the importance of just being you, in whatever circumstances. A young lad (about 2 years old) was in the garden, riding an imaginary horse. His grandfather was watching him, and as the young lad dismounted, Granddad asked: 'What's your horse's name?'

'Bullseye,' replied the boy.

'So you must be Woody then,' reasoned Granddad, who had taken great care to notice this when watching *Toy Story 2* with his grandson.

'No,' said the boy, looking confused.

'Oh, well who are you then?' asked Granddad.

'I'm Ben!' said the boy – for that was indeed his name.

'Oh, I guess Woody must have loaned his horse to you,' said Granddad.

'Yes,' said Ben.

At this point everyone who had overheard the conversation roared with laughter. You see, for Ben this was a ridiculous question. Ben was Ben. Why should he be anyone else? I guess we should all be a bit more childlike every now and again and remember who we are, too.

You're a Person, not a Job Title

Another misconception many people have is to believe that they are defined by what they do – they will tell you that they are 'an engineer' or 'a lawyer' or 'an architect'. In fact, our occupations are simply things that 'occupy' our time.

I know that it can be difficult to disengage sometimes when we are in the middle of a big crisis at work; but if we don't, we run the risk of adding to the problem rather than being objective enough to solve it. As you will see in the next chapter, your job is really only one part of who you are and even who you want to be. By all means do your job well, provide value for the money you earn, but don't make the mistake of confusing your job with your life. Everything in life happens too quickly to devote it to just one thing; seasons change, children grow up, relationships wither from lack of nourishment and even skills deteriorate with a lack of repetition. You need to pay attention to all areas of your life. If you use this book to do more in your life, dwell on this chapter and on Chapter 2 to understand why you choose to do the things you do.

I once heard a story about a woman who listened to her husband for hours each night as he 'dumped', in minute detail, the problems and trivial issues that had arisen at work that day. She heard all about the office politics, the number of times the photocopier had jammed, the countless times he had been frustrated by suppliers, distributors and clients, and even the temperature of the water cooler. One night, in the middle of a story about some trivial incident, she decided that she could not take any more and very quietly she got up and left. He probably didn't even notice her leaving. In the case notes presented by her lawyers in the ensuing divorce she included an invoice for 10 000 hours of time devoted to her husband's job over the 12 years they had been married.

Now I don't know if this story is true, but I do know that it is not an isolated example. Millions of people across the world go through the same ritual every day – why? I think it is because we identify too closely with what we do instead of who we are. We fear that unless we talk at length about our jobs we will not be a significant person in the eyes of those around us. We are all greater than the sum of the hours we spend working – whatever we do. Certainly, we should discuss what has happened today if it is interesting, but keep it brief. Don't work for 8 hours, relive it for 4 hours and then prepare for the next session. Get home and start focusing on the other things in your life, like your partner, your children, their interests, your hobbies and that exercise that you have been putting off for the last 2 years due to time pressures.

ACTIVITY

Tell your partner that just for the next 30 days, you will only give one of the following three responses as a summary of your working day when you get home:

- **'Good'**
- **'Fair'**
- **'It's not worth regurgitating'**

After 30 days, you can elaborate a bit more – but only if something really significant (and of genuine interest to your partner) has occurred.

I know this is going to be one of the most difficult tasks in this book for some of you and you will probably need some alternative topics to discuss, or activities to do. So here are some ideas:

- Discuss items of interest that you've read about today.
- Play a game with your family.
- Discuss interesting ideas that you've had.
- Help your kids with their assignments.
- Tell your partner about people you met during your working hours.
- Go for a walk.
- Visit some relatives or friends.
- Read a book.
- Listen to music.
- Do some physical activity.
- Relax – now there's a thought!

Do this for a month and you'll be amazed at how much time you will have to get on with other important things in your life.

You are Everything . . . and Everything is You

I would contend that you, the person reading this book, are a unique combination. Right now, your uniqueness is comprised of the following:

- Your physical state
- Your spiritual state
- Your circumstances
- Your environment
- The times in which you live

This combination of time and place is sufficient for us to understand that right now we should be having the time of our lives – and if you are not, why not?

ACTIVITY

Take 5 minutes now to think through the things about you that make you unique. Write them down and then rank them in order of importance so that the number one item is the one that most people that you know would identify immediately as being YOU. Now, during the course of the next week find an opportunity every day to demonstrate this unique quality.

Too often we do not utilize our individuality and the result is wasted energy trying to fit into a different, perhaps more acceptable, mould. In reality, when you start acting in ways that emphasize your uniqueness, acceptance from the people around you increases. You will become more relaxed and make other people feel more at ease. This, in turn, facilitates better communication and makes every interaction you have more time effective.

Are you having the time of your life?

One of my dad's many sayings is: 'We're only here once, so make sure you make the most of it.' From a time management perspective, this translates into maximizing the value you get from every moment that you are alive. To do this, you need to understand the value of each small increment of time and have a meaningful appreciation of the nature of risk so that you can move forward without fear.

Every Breath You Take

If you have ever wondered how much you could do with your time, try holding your breath for 60 seconds while looking at your watch. Isn't it astounding how many things you can think about, how many things you can see in a minute? Now, do the same thing, but hold your breath for 65 seconds. Isn't it amazing how long those last 5 seconds take to go by? Every breath you take is a measure of your time on the planet, so make the most of each one. Too many people live their lives waiting for the perfect circumstances before they commit to doing anything:

'When my job gets a little less demanding I'm going to spend some time with my family.'

Or the really intriguing one:

'I'll get started on my exercise programme as soon as I lose some weight.'

Let's face facts. There will never be enough time to do everything and there will also never be a time when everything will be perfect. The only 'right time' is the time at which action is taken and the people who move forward are those who get started and mould the circumstances to fit their requirements. Invariably, such activity induces something I like to call Simes' Law of Serendipity:[1]

❛ An open door is an open invitation. ❜

I think it runs off the tongue a little easier than the alternative: 'Before opening your door, wait for people to queue outside to see if they can help with the project that you may be undertaking even though they're not quite sure what it is you are doing.'

When you take action (open the door) you invite all sorts of people to get involved in your projects and they can do so because they can see what you are doing. The contribution of others will vary from verbal encouragement through to physical, mental and emotional help to get you to the finishing post quickly and effectively. Activity is the key and is also the reason why successful people benefit from momentum in their lives and in their

---

[1] All my friends call me Simes.

businesses. In Chapter 5 I will describe the Results Cyclone, but for now why don't you commit to opening your door more often – who knows who will pop in?

The Greatest Risk of All

❝ The risk of riskless living is the greatest risk of all. ❞   Stephen Covey

Covey's sentence is beautiful and encapsulates so much. Many people fear all sorts of things and take so few risks in life. Consequently, their lives become full of worry, trying to find other ways to achieve things that the more 'risky' ways would have achieved in much less time. Fear can hold you back in so many ways – and it really is no more than False Evidence Appearing Real – so give it no power in your life and start having the time of your life. Take some risks and accept no excuses from yourself – that way you'll have no regrets.

It's rude to point

The complaint I hear most often when I introduce the topic of time management to senior management groups is: 'If only we could get our people to accept more responsibility, it would save us all a lot of time.'

The issue is that rather than focus on finding a solution to a problem, people prefer to look for scapegoats. So, to help you avoid this time-sapping, energy-busting habit – which is said to be the cause of 90 per cent of the time management issues we face – let me introduce to you a truism that has helped cure many: you should never point a finger of blame at someone else because you will always have three fingers pointing back at the person who is probably more responsible for the problem – you.

ACTIVITY

Point the Finger

Try this game for fun with your friends and family.

1. **Jot down one situation when someone else was to blame for something that happened to you.**

2. Read your situation out to the group while pointing your index finger at them.

3. Ask every person to think of at least three reasons why the actual problem could have been:

A. Caused by you

B. Avoided by you

C. Alleviated by you

D. Unavoidable and therefore no-one was to blame

4. While the other people are talking you should remain silent.

5. Have fun with this exercise; don't get involved in blaming situations, just analyse where things could have been different.

You can do this exercise on your own if you are willing to suspend self-interest and do some 'possibility thinking'. Once you have thought of a situation, put yourself in the place of one of the people staring at your pointed finger and try to think how they could have been helped to avoid making the mistake. What else could you have done to change their course of action? What may have caused them to respond as they did? What physical and organizational restrictions do they wrestle with? Sometimes, thinking through how you would do things differently next time provides some insight into the potential causes of the problem.

When we have done this with groups on our training courses it is amazing how many reasons people come up with as to why the person pointing the finger was probably more at fault than the people being accused. I think so many answers are generated because we live in a 'blame culture' and we are constantly being challenged to defend ourselves against ridiculous accusations from individuals refusing to accept responsibility for their own actions (or sometimes their inactivity).

The key lesson here is obvious: before you look to pass the buck, lay the blame or find a fault, look at the three fingers below your forward-pointing finger and consider whether they are telling you something. The benefits from a time management perspective are significant, for accepting personal responsibility can lead to all sorts of opportunities:

- You can save time and effort by forgetting the incident and moving on.

- You can learn more by assessing the situation and understanding how to avoid a recurrence.

- You will gain the respect of those around you as you will be perceived as refreshingly 'different'.

- You can focus on creating a solution to the problem.

- You will engender trust and receive assistance from your colleagues and friends as they will not need to 'defend themselves' whenever you are around.

- Your chances of promotion will soar as all leaders know the value of accepting responsibility.

At the beginning of the chapter I posed the question 'Why do successful people seem to get more done than others?' Well, successful people do not dwell on issues that are not contributing to their goals. Pointing fingers and moaning about personal circumstances are a waste of time and energy. If you are guilty of this – and, let's be honest, we are all guilty of this sometimes – why not use your time more effectively and work on finding a solution to your problems?

Think Positive

While we are being honest, doesn't it feel better, and healthier, to be working on something positively rather than tearing the world apart, one infinitesimally small piece at a time? A good example would be a traffic jam. Here are the ways some of my friends dealt with this 'feature' of western society recently – can you spot the person struggling with responsibility?

'I hate to stand still so I came off the motorway and took a slightly longer route. I saw some beautiful scenery.'

'There was a delay on the way here so I was able to listen to the whole programme.'

'I don't believe it. Every time I get on the motorway, someone decides to have an accident.'

You don't have to do everything

Many people confuse responsibility with needing to do everything themselves. But, in the words of George Gershwin, 'it ain't necessarily so'. You can retain responsibility while asking other people to do things for you or just accepting offers of help.

I had an opportunity to put this into practice while writing this book. The contract for the book arrived on my doorstep when my wife was 6 months pregnant and we were in the middle of moving home. As is usual with such events, our moving date coincided with the predicted birth date and as a result we were in danger of being overwhelmed by the enormity of the tasks in hand. Our parents volunteered to help out in any way they could, but initially, our response, being human, was to decline the kind offer, insisting that we would cope. However, as the date moved closer it became obvious that help was what we needed most. It was 'all hands on deck', with everyone moving furniture, unpacking boxes, washing surfaces and generally getting the job done. Actually, the hardest job was forcing my heavily pregnant wife to sit down and relax – but, thankfully, the mums were extremely persuasive!

Afterwards, I reflected on why it is that we typically decline offers of help even when it is the most sensible choice available to us. I decided it was probably for one of these reasons:

- We don't like others to think that we cannot cope.
- We don't wish to impose on others.

Let's take a closer look at these because they have a lot more impact than our ability to delegate – they influence the way that we think about our lives. First of all, the feeling that others are assessing our ability to cope stems from two potential sources – poor self-confidence and high self-consciousness. Regardless of the psychobabble that surrounds these tendencies, they create the same need – to present a facade of invincibility. Outwardly, people with these dispositions seem to cope with anything that life throws at them and still come out smiling. The truth behind the facade is somewhat different, though; and the decline into mental and physical health problems can be both swift and dramatic. Someone should tell these people that life is not supposed to be this hard. Indeed, it might be a good idea to tie them up for a few days and force them to relax. It is a truism that it takes two to tango; and it is people working together or in teams who achieve most of the major breakthroughs in history and in life.

The second reason for not accepting help is one that I have battled with for years. I hate to feel that I am 'imposing' on others. Consequently, I will go out of my way to do something or meet a commitment even when my diary is starting to look like a bus timetable of appointments. If you are like this, try asking yourself how you feel when you offer help to someone close to you and they turn you down. At the risk of being too dramatic, it can be devastating, can't it? Now, imagine how you may be making others feel when you constantly turn down their offers of help. The truth is that people like to help – it makes them feel better. So, let them. Just be sure to thank them sincerely afterwards and all of a sudden life becomes that little bit better.

KEY POINTS

- ⊷ We all have the same amount of time in a day; successful people use their time more effectively
- ⊷ You are unique and you have a unique contribution to make to the world
- ⊷ It is only by taking some risks that we move forward in life. Undue caution will rob you of some of life's greatest opportunities
- ⊷ Taking responsibility for what happens in your life is the quickest route to success in any endeavour
- ⊷ Accepting help is an act of maturity and grace.

So, now that you know who you are, you are halfway towards completing the foundations upon which you can build your time management skills. Next, let's find out what you really want out of life so that you can utilize the magnificent power of motivation.

2 Live, Love, Learn, Leave a Legacy – define your own life balance

There are four key areas to life – Live, Love, Learn and Leave a Legacy. Your mission, should you wish to accept it, is to find your own balance. As an absolute minimum, you should at least consider all four areas before you finish your forward planning. Then, if you still have a diary that is full with no room for time for exercise, at least it will be a conscious decision. The purpose of this chapter is to help you think about YOU. What do you want to have, do and become? You will use key areas to structure your thoughts, and these will cover all areas of your life. However, some aspects of your life may well fit into a number of different areas – for example, for some people, spiritual beliefs will have an impact on all key areas of their lives, and this is okay. Just ensure that when you come to construct your Life Map – described later in this chapter – you capture your thoughts in every area.

Before we go too far, though, grab a pencil and complete the question-naire on pp. 20–21. It will give you an idea of how your life is balanced currently.

Personal Life Balance Questionnaire

Answer all questions by writing the appropriate number in the box provided, using the following scale:

Rarely or never true = 1   Some of the time = 2   Most of the time = 3   All of the time = 4

	Rarely or never true (1)	Some of the time (2)	Most of the time (3)	All of the time (4)
1 My inboxes are clear (email / voicemail / paper)	☐	☐	☐	☐
2 I am in control of the information I need	☐	☐	☐	☐
3 I spend quality time with my family	☐	☐	☐	☐
4 I make time for hobbies and interests	☐	☐	☐	☐
5 I follow a regular exercise plan	☐	☐	☐	☐
6 I spend 'quiet' time with my partner	☐	☐	☐	☐
7 I plan my television viewing	☐	☐	☐	☐
8 I get enough sleep	☐	☐	☐	☐
9 I make time to read	☐	☐	☐	☐
10 I am up to date with what is happening in the world	☐	☐	☐	☐
11 I read quality books to learn new things	☐	☐	☐	☐
12 I make time for fun	☐	☐	☐	☐
13 I never say 'I haven't got time'	☐	☐	☐	☐
14 I make time to spend with friends	☐	☐	☐	☐
15 I pay bills on time	☐	☐	☐	☐

16	I take regular holidays	☐	☐	☐	☐
17	I remember important events	☐	☐	☐	☐
18	I remember birthdays and anniversaries	☐	☐	☐	☐
19	I never lose important information	☐	☐	☐	☐
20	I am organized	☐	☐	☐	☐
21	I am focused	☐	☐	☐	☐
22	Personal development is key to me	☐	☐	☐	☐
23	I watch educational / informational programmes	☐	☐	☐	☐
24	I attend seminars and other learning events	☐	☐	☐	☐
25	I am always on time	☐	☐	☐	☐
26	I like to prioritize events and activities	☐	☐	☐	☐
27	I have high energy levels	☐	☐	☐	☐
28	I have my goals written down	☐	☐	☐	☐
29	I find it easy to say 'No'	☐	☐	☐	☐
30	I am working on my life goals	☐	☐	☐	☐
TOTALS		☐	☐	☐	☐

Calculate your overall score by adding together the totals of the four columns.

My Personal Life Balance score is : ☐

Personal Life Balance questionnaire – implications

Overall

30–60 points   It would seem that time management is not one of your core skills! This book could be a revelation to you.

61–90 points   Either you are being very modest or you are being dishonest. Alternatively, you could be one of the many people that would like to be good at time management but have never succeeded using traditional methods and tools.

91–120 points   Thank you for volunteering to teach one of our courses. Actually, you will probably have a lot of fun updating your skills with this book.

Life Areas

Add up your scores for the four key life areas below. Then use the formula to determine your effectiveness in each area:

Live (questions 4, 5, 7, 8, 12, 16, 26, 27, 28, 29, 30)

Formula: your score / 44 × 100   [   ]%

Love (questions 3, 6, 13, 14, 18)

Formula: your score / 20 × 100   [   ]%

Learn (questions 9, 10, 11, 22, 23, 24)

Formula: your score / 24 × 100   [   ]%

Leave a Legacy (questions 1, 2, 15, 17, 19, 20, 21, 25)

Formula: your score / 32 × 100   [   ]%

There are no right or wrong scores to achieve in this exercise. The key to interpreting your effectiveness in each area is to assess the balance. Are your life areas in balance? If not, are you happy with the scores? Do any of them surprise you? If you are happy, is there room for improvement on a personal level? The rest of this chapter will delve in detail into a range of possibilities for each life area – and you will have many more to add. Your task is to keep working on your personal life balance so that you can begin to live a life tailored to your individual requirements.

At the end of this book, you will see another copy of the Personal Life Balance Questionnaire. What I would like you to do is to complete the second questionnaire after you have been implementing the actions and suggestions in this book for about a month. Typically, it takes about 30 days to acquire a new habit, so that should be sufficient to assess how well you are doing against your own targets. Keep using the questionnaire until you are living the life you want to lead.

Let's take a look at each of the four key areas in detail now. Try not to concentrate too much on the examples used – think more about your own requirements. I have included lots of examples to stimulate your mind and help you when you come to the next activity.

Live

Imagine you had at your disposal 24 hours a day, 7 days a week, 365 days a year, for the rest of your life . . . what would you do? Oh, and money is no object.

For many people, the list would be almost infinite, starting with a round-the-world trip and continuing with endless fun activities and spending sprees. For others, the list would be simpler, focusing on health and leisurely pursuits. Whatever your list includes, this is the life area that covers your dreams. The types of items considered here include travel, your health, sport and entertainment, accommodation and material possessions.

Travel

When considering your life areas it is important to be as thorough as possible. When my wife and I completed this exercise, for example, we calculated that we would need approximately 96 years to visit all the places on our travel list. How would you like to go on a fishing trip to Alaska? How about a walk along the Great Wall of China or a flight into space? Even this last item is now possible if you are wealthy enough. Remember, your thinking here should not be constrained by your current situation; in many respects this is a dream session in which you will uncover some thoughts that last filled your head when you were still in school. Just go with the flow – be guided by your intuition rather than your mind.

Health

If you could inhabit the body of any living person, who would it be? What is it about their physique that attracts you? Okay, now take this a step further. How do you think this individual treats their body on a daily basis? Do they eat regular, healthy meals? Do they exercise? Do they have time to relax and tune in to their bodies? Do they get enough sleep to recharge the batteries? So, now you need to decide if you would like to work towards this ideal. Again, assume you have 24 hours a day at your disposal, what would you like to do in the health area? Would you like to run a few miles a day, swim for 30 minutes, complete a regular workout at the gym or just go for an energetic walk every morning? Would you have your own gym and a personal trainer? Would your swimming pool be indoor, outdoor or at the local sports centre? What about your diet? Would you like your body to be a temple or a deli? The choice is yours. My mother-in-law has told me that she would like to retire just so that she could spend more time in the kitchen cooking some of her favourite cakes. The bad news is that I love her cooking – the good news is that she has not retired yet. One of my dreams is to eat my way around the world. I love eating authentic foods, cooked in the country of their origin using traditional methods – how about you?

Sport and Entertainment

Would you like to see the Olympic Games live or maybe follow your nation's team through each stage of the World Cup? If you prefer to play rather than spectate, how about playing golf at St Andrews or Augusta? Have you ever wanted to ski in Canada or sail around the Cape? Would you like to learn some new sports, such as horse riding or archery? Your idea of fun might be a week trekking around the foothills of the Rockies or maybe even hang-gliding in the Alps.

When it comes to entertainment, what would you like to see, do and experience? Is there a band you've always wanted to see live but now they are so big they only play a few live dates a year (in exotic locations)? Why not add it to your list anyway? Maybe live theatre is your dream, watching the latest Lloyd Webber production in London's West End or perhaps seeing *Chicago* on Broadway. If 'Life is a Cabaret', when's the next performance in your life?

Accommodation

If money were indeed no object, where would you live? What type of property would you choose? Would it be based in the countryside and have land or would it be an apartment overlooking the city? For those of you who like playing on computers, there are some great software titles that take you through the process of designing your ideal home, step by step. I did one of these recently and it was fantastic. You decide how many rooms you will have, the overall layout, which rooms will overlook the garden, where the pool, jacuzzi, steam-room and the bar will be situated, how big the kitchen will be, the size of the bedrooms and en-suite bathrooms, the number of guests you will be able to entertain at your dining table, the scale of the games room, the positioning of the speakers for your total home sound system, the shape and grandeur of the staircase, and that's all before you start the decorating. Don't forget to think outside the box again. What will your land contain? Will there be stables or a wildlife sanctuary? Will there be room for a tennis court or two or maybe a full-sized basketball court? Is your property situated at the end of a long gravel drive or on an island? The key, as I am sure you are beginning to notice, is that you are the chief architect for your future – you decide.

Things

Okay, so you've got your home designed, but what vehicles would be parked outside? Executive saloons, the latest sports car or any old jalopy as long as it got you from A to B? What 'toys' would you have? A snooker table, a private cinema or maybe your own music studio? When it comes to 'things' the list can be as long and as individual as there are people in the world. The important thing to remember is that every idea or whimsical fancy that springs to mind is valid – even if it is something that you decided long ago was just not going to happen for you. Some categories that might prompt you in the development of your own list are:

- Clothes
- Kitchen gadgets
- Cars and motorbikes
- Dining-room essentials
- Electronic gadgets
- Jewellery
- Antiques

- Wine collection
- Planes and boats
- Art
- Sporting equipment
- Furniture
- Books
- Hobbies

Some people get quite upset when discussing this particular area, arguing that it is incredibly materialistic. In some respects they are absolutely correct, of course – we are discussing material items. All I would say is that if you feel you can hit all your personal requirements in this area with just a few basics, that's great. It may be that your Life Map will contain much more substance when we come to discuss the other areas – Love, Learn and Leave a Legacy.

For now, though, it is important to be as open-minded and creative as possible while you are thinking about your dreams. Later in the chapter we will be creating your Life Map and this will be your opportunity to begin the process of designing your future.

Love

This key area is built on a foundation of relationships. Who are the people that mean the most to you in life? Construct a list in your mind. You may wish to think initially of your partner and your family before extending out to other relatives and close friends. Once you are satisfied that the list is reasonably comprehensive, let your mind wander and capture everything that is important to you. The following may help.

Partner

Would you be more romantic, if only you had the time? Well, for a moment, pretend that you do have the time. Where would you take your partner? What would you do? Would you just stay in, hire someone to prepare and serve a meal for you both, preceded by champagne, accompanied by fine wine and followed by exotic liqueurs from around the world? Or would you dine out at the finest restaurants with a chauffeur taking the responsibility for getting you home – when you are completely satisfied?

Maybe travel is your thing. How many of the destinations in your 'Live' key area are a dream for both of you? How long would each trip be? Would the trips be a surprise or would the excitement be even greater for you both if you planned it all together?

If money were no object, what would you like to buy for your partner? Would it be expensive jewellery, exotic perfumes, designer outfits, clothes that are in fashion rather than in the sale? Or would your partner be the proud owner of their favourite car on their next birthday?

What life experiences would you like to share? Would you like to take your kids to Lapland at Christmas or your partner to the carnival in Rio? If you want to get 'steamy', how about the Orient Express? Perhaps a picnic of fruit and wine on Table Mountain in Cape Town would capture your imagination?

Maybe the big thing for you two would just be 'time' – time to breathe, time to talk, time to just . . . be together.

Family

How much time do you spend with your parents, your grandparents, your brothers and sisters, your children, your grandchildren? When I ask senior executives this question, it is as if a light goes on in their heads and they realize that they are spending very little time with the people they love most. Now this may not be the case for you; if so, move on to the next section. However, if family is important to you – use this exercise as an opportunity to capture some of the things you'd like to do and share with them. I once heard that life was all about making memories – what memories would you like to recollect when you look back on your life? Typically, as we rush around attempting to provide for our loved ones, we overlook the opportunities to build the relationships that will make the future secure and fulfilling. By the time we retire, our kids are strangers, our parents have passed away and we are living empty and lonely lives. Many books published in the 1980s and 1990s encouraged us to spend 'quality time' with our loved ones – as if this would compensate for the diminishing amount of time we were spending with them. However, more recent research has shown that we need to spend time in 'quantity' with our loved ones in order to develop the relationship effectively. Of course, the truth, as so often in life, is that a balance is needed. There is no point spending a lot of time in the presence of our families if all we are going to do is watch television. Similarly, quality conversations do not develop if they are prompted only once a week. We need time to build rapport and to understand the people we seek to engage. Think back to the last time you met someone who captured your heart. Did you just arrange to meet up with them a month later and not contact them in the interim? I doubt it. I suspect that you made every attempt to see or talk to them daily (if not more frequently than that). When we focus on something or someone, we devote an appropriate amount of time and energy to do the job properly. It is only complacency that leads to anything less.

Would you like to tell a different story? Great. Don't worry too much about the 'how', just capture the 'what' of your closest relationships. What would you like to do with your family? How often would you call them if you had the time? What surprises would you like to present to them? What sports and hobbies would you like to do with them? Do you know their deepest wants? What dreams do they have? Could you share those dreams and get involved in making them happen?

Friends

It's said you can't choose your family but you can choose your friends. For this reason, many people consider the relationships they have with friends to be among their most valued. However, how many times have you found yourself writing Christmas or other holiday cards and saying: 'I really should get in touch with them'? Again, suspend reality for a few minutes and consider what you would like to do with some of your key friends. Would you like to share holidays with them? Where would you go? Would you take the children if you have any? How long would you stay? Would you love to spend New Year with them on a Scottish island, relaxing by the coal fire, drinking hot drinks and whisky, playing games and generally having fun? Maybe an activity holiday would be more up your street – skiing in the Alps, scuba-diving on the Great Barrier Reef, walking through the Amazonian forests. Perhaps you would prefer to absorb the culture and splendour of Rome or discover the diversity and mystique of India? Or could it be that a regular arrangement just to meet up and share a few hours socially would be of real value to you? Whatever it is, set your mind free and capture your ideas and thoughts.

Learn

❝ The secret to life is to constantly grow. ❞   Anthony Robbins

I am constantly amazed at the number of people attending our digital time management course who have not read an educational book since they left school. It may well be that our educational system in the UK fails to build the desire for lifelong learning in our children; however, I understand from my clients and colleagues around the world that this is not a challenge limited to the confines of my own country. Someone once said that 'school is never out for the professional', and when I look at the most successful people that I know, I see that they are united in their zest for knowledge, their enthusiasm to learn new concepts and their urge to develop new skills. We are surrounded by opportunities to learn. What would you like to do if you had 24 hours a day to focus on your personal development? How would you choose to develop your 'mental muscles'?

Books, E-books and the Internet

Finding something good to read is incredibly easy these days. Indeed, once you make it a habit, it is quite difficult to avoid creating a backlog of interesting material to read. We will investigate some of the excellent sources of literature later, but for now, why don't you consider some of the areas that you would like to know more about or books you would like to have read? To get you started here are some categories that our students have created on our courses – feel free to edit or add to this list:

- 'How to' books (you name them)
- Religious texts
- Scientific journals
- Local, national and international history
- Shakespeare's complete works

- Hobbies and interests
- Business books
- Art and culture
- Biology and natural history
- Technology manuals
- Great literary texts
- Ancient Greek mythology
- Space exploration

Traditionally, libraries and book shops were the first places to go for anything written. Now, the Internet would probably be the first port of call for many people, whether it is to find or order a book or to download an e-book. E-books are a fantastic way of accessing literature from anywhere without taking up valuable luggage space. Most come in relatively small files and can be downloaded to your handheld computer, your laptop or even your mobile phone.

Many of the younger delegates on our courses argue that they learn all they want from television through programmes on the Discovery Channel or documentaries. However, without understanding too much about the way the brain works, I still think reading is a more effective way to learn for a number of reasons:

1. It is interactive (your brain interprets the information).
2. It stimulates the imagination in a way television cannot.
3. Written material is open to interpretation.
4. Bias and misinformation can be challenged through reading around a subject and assessing the information provided by several different authors.

Nevertheless, television can still provide a useful starting point and is very good at stimulating the desire to find out more on a given topic.

Audio

There are times when reading a book or researching on the Internet are just not practical for one of two reasons:

1. You are doing something that requires your full conscious attention (like driving).

2. It is not the best method for learning something (like a new language).

My car is like a mobile university, with tapes all over the front passenger seat. It is amazing how much you can learn on the journey to work, or on the longer trips to visit friends and family.

Now let's say that your typical journey to work is just 30 minutes – how much could you learn just by switching off the radio and listening to a teaching programme instead? 5 hours a week (including the return journey) for 50 weeks is a lot – actually, it's 250 hours! What new skills would you like to learn in that time?

- A new language
- Essential business skills like effective communication, delegation, negotiation and a host of other '-ations'
- Selling skills
- The basics of a new hobby or interest

It is estimated that this level of study would make you one of the leading world experts in your chosen field within 5 years. Certainly, just by doing this a couple of days a week you will differentiate yourself from about 95 per cent of your colleagues – would that be of use to you professionally?

As you think through some of the things you could learn, do consider the home study courses that are available on tape or CD-ROM. Another category available as audio books is popular biography – usually, this condensed format makes them more accessible. Most biographies in written format are several hundred pages long, whereas in audio format they are concentrated into about an hour. Biographies are an excellent source of ideas and, more importantly, examples of great attitudes (see 'Other People' later in this chapter).

Seminars and Open Programmes

Nothing generates more excitement and enthusiasm than a live event that is facilitated skilfully. The live circuit is awash with powerful business speakers and enlightened educators; all you have to do is sign up for a few of them.

What takes your fancy? Would you like to attend the latest business seminars for your industry or perhaps brush up on your knowledge of a related industry at an exhibition? Why not do some research and find out where your favourite speaker is appearing? Most accomplished public speakers have their own website with details of their forthcoming bookings. Failing that, most industries have trade magazines that publish details of forthcoming events. Is there a training course that you've always wanted to attend? How about a thrilling training extravaganza on digital time management? I hear there is an excellent course in that field! Seriously, many government agencies and local bodies have created whole curricula for the likes of you and me – why not make use of them? It's not like school; in fact, every attempt is made to make adult classes as interactive, energetic and as fun as possible. If nothing springs to mind straight away, but you think you might be interested in attending some classes to broaden your knowledge, just note your intent for now and fill in the gaps after you have done your research. Believe me, nothing is more powerful than a live event because you are completely focused on what is being said. When you read a book or listen to a CD there are constant interruptions; when you attend a seminar or a training event you can immerse yourself in the atmosphere, internalize the message and energize your spirit.

Here's a list of secondary benefits you can hope to experience at a live event:

- Fun – everyone attending is a volunteer, so the general atmosphere is one of determination to enjoy the experience.
- New friends – what better way to meet like-minded people than to attend an event aimed at people just like you?
- Boosted learning – the potent mixture of sight, sound, atmosphere and group desire to learn delivers an experience unlike any other in the educational arena.
- Greater insight – speakers at big events generally divulge more of themselves than they can possibly hope to achieve through the written word.
- Deeper commitment – as indicated earlier, there is something about attending a seminar that captivates a part of your psyche untouched by more traditional forms of training – try it and see.

- Coached by champions – I have experienced an immense burst of energy and determination to achieve my goals and dreams after various live events with great inspirational speakers like Anthony Robbins, Frank Dick, Chris Bonnington and Heather Mills.

Skills

I have a friend who makes a new year resolution that really inspires him. For the last 8 years he has committed himself to learning a new skill every year. To date, he has learned the following:

1. Hang-gliding
2. Playing chess
3. Glider piloting
4. Watercolour painting
5. Computer basics
6. Clay shooting
7. Baking
8. Motorcycling

I believe that he is currently learning how to play golf. Having hit a ball around a few golf courses in my time, I have suggested that he extends this resolution to at least 20 years, but he is content that he is making good progress. The other remarkable thing about this guy is that he is nearly 69 years old!

I tell you this story because I think it demonstrates two key points:

1. You're never too old to learn new things.
2. To succeed in anything you need to apply focus.

However, for the purposes of this exercise, all you need to do is consider some of the skills you would like to acquire. Is there something you have been putting off for years that would really excite you? Maybe there is something from your youth that you'd like to restart? Perhaps there is something that you'd like to do with your partner, like sailing or trekking? How about learning to cook? There are some great holidays you can go on that combine the acquisition of a new skill with beautiful and sunny surroundings like painting in Italy, cooking in Spain or photography in Africa. Would any of these interest you?

Other People

Without a doubt, the greatest source of knowledge and experience that you could tap into is all around you. 'Other people' form the most important skill and knowledge base that you could ever need. There is probably not one problem or challenge that you face that has not been considered, at least in part, by someone else. All you have to do is seek them out. It makes sense to model what works, and by that I mean why spend your time trying to work out how to do something when there are people all around you that have already achieved it and could help you do the same.

Are there some groups that you would like to join to expand your horizons? Most big towns and cities have speaking groups that are run on a voluntary basis and are always open to new members. Then there are business associations, industry bodies, interest groups, pressure groups and lobbyists – is there an issue you'd like to know more about?

Perhaps you learn better in a one-to-one environment where you can get to the heart of an issue and discuss it openly? If so, why not seek out a like-minded individual, maybe someone who has already achieved some of the things you would like to emulate, and ask them to be your mentor? If this sounds too formal, why not arrange to meet up with them for a coffee or lunch and you pay? I can assure you that most people will be flattered by the gesture and you will get more than the price of a sandwich in value from your friend. Make sure to ask if it would be okay to take notes during the meeting – you never know when you might need some of the information you pick up. When you meet, ask lots of open questions and let them do the talking. After all, if they were there to listen to you, they would be paying. Apply the golden rules of communication – listen, listen and listen again.

I know that some of you will be in a business where you have regular access to an adviser or a mentor. All I would say is, be thankful because you will always get more from those sessions than them. They are giving up time that could have been devoted to their personal goals but instead they are working with you to help you achieve yours. The best way to repay them is to follow their advice.

Leave a Legacy

You may be one of those people that have achieved most of their dreams and goals already and if so, you may be wondering, 'Is that it? There must be more to life than just setting goals and then achieving them.' Well, that is what this area of your life is all about. What do you want people to remember about you? Is it that you were a kind, honest person or someone who dedicated their life to improving the lives of others? What are you attempting to build in your life? Is it a secure family environment or is it a level of wealth that means your family will never need to work again? When do you plan to retire? Is it when you reach the official retirement age or when you are in a position not to need an income from a job any more? What would you like to give back to society? Are you happy with regular donations to your favourite charity or would you like to commit time and energy to that same charity?

The Tombstone test should help you to focus. Stated simply the Tombstone test is 'What would you wish people to write on your tombstone?'. Your legacy will be there for everyone to see – what will it say?

Let's take a look at just some of the things you may wish to consider in this key area.

Job

Why do you work? This is such a basic question and yet one that most people cannot really answer beyond the instinctive 'to earn money'. We spend nearly 50 per cent of our waking hours, and sometimes much more, doing something that we are unable to justify. Sure, earning money is important if you want to do other things – from basic needs such as eating and sleeping comfortably through to extravagant requirements such as exotic holidays and elaborate jewellery. My question to you is: 'What would be enough money for you?' You need to know the answer to this question – precisely. If your answer is, for example, twice the amount you currently earn then you need to look for other ways of making money. Conversely, if it is exactly half what you are earning currently then you could consider doing less or something completely different that is paid less.

The point I am making is that too often we find ourselves moaning about our circumstances as if we were powerless to change them: 'I've only had one day off in the last three weeks', 'This job makes me sick, I can't believe some of the people I have to work with!', 'I'm tired of getting up at 5 every morning'. This is your opportunity to think 'outside of the box', so use it wisely. What job would you do if you had the right skills, experience, connections, qualifications, financial circumstances? In an ideal world would you have a job at all? Where would you work if you had the chance? How many days a week would you prefer to work?

This last question is one that we ask frequently at work–life balance programmes, and once people have had time to think about it, they usually say that four days would be nice so that they can have longer weekends with their families or weekends away with their friends. The surprise for many of them is that this is usually possible by compressing their work hours and measuring results instead of processes. The amazing thing is that often what we would like is only one good question away. Why not write down what you would like? Who knows what could happen.

The one thing that many of you will notice when you create your Life Map is that, despite the fact that your job is so pervasive in your life, it is only one item on your whole map, tucked away in the corner. For some of you workaholics out there, I hope the number of items elsewhere on your map will convince you that there can be more to life than the job.

Multiple Streams of Income

There has been a shift in working patterns in recent years. The number of people who have just one job or rely on one stream of income has declined dramatically. More and more people are recognizing that there is only limited security in any job. They have learnt that even the most prestigious corporate giants are not immune to the vagaries of the marketplace, not to mention the activities of their directors and accountants! Meanwhile, some of those within jobs continue as if nothing has changed. This approach to the task of long-term income generation is haphazard at best. Indeed, despite the fact that retirement funds are rapidly dwindling as pensioners begin to outnumber the people entering the tax-generating ranks, many people are continuing to live without even the most basic levels of long-term insurance and income. Daily, the news is full of the latest factory closures and major corporation redundancies. So, what are you doing about it? Are you tackling the issue head-on or are you putting your head in the sand and hoping that you win the lottery this week?

As you will see later in this book, opportunities abound for those willing to step out and work for them. Why not use the same technology that has created many of our greatest challenges to generate second and even third incomes for yourself? Perhaps you would prefer to branch out into a new area and develop a completely new set of skills in your spare time so that you can start your own business one day? Who knows? But if you are one of those people we discussed earlier who would like to earn more but whose capacity in their current job is limited, maybe you should add some ideas to this section of your Life Map.

Investments

Anyone who knows me will be relieved to hear that I am not about to give you some financial advice or recommend an investment strategy that will transform your life. I am very good at getting focused on earning money, but when it comes to making that money work for me I seek professional help from people who know what they are talking about and enjoy figures. However, I do recognize that one option for people looking to develop an additional stream of income is to invest it. Whether you decide to invest in rental property or the latest high-tech stocks, there are ways of getting your money to work for you when you are asleep (a concept that keeps me awake at night, which is not supposed to be the idea). Anyway, the bottom line is: what are you looking to do in this area – what is your strategy? Are you looking for a regular income or capital growth? Will you be happy to have enough stashed away so that when you choose to retire your lifestyle will remain unchanged, or are you looking to build up enough money to enable you to retire in a few years' time? Whatever you decide, be sure to seek out good advice. I have found that referrals in this field are like gold dust. If a trusted friend can recommend a good all-round adviser, go with the recommendation rather than be influenced by a stack of letters after a name or industry credentials.

Charity and the Community

Enough about your needs – what would you like to give back to the world? It has become fashionable to think that charities only need help at certain times of the year when they launch their respective television campaigns. This could not be further from the truth. Everyone that I have met that works in the charitable sector tells me that while there is no real shortage of people looking to help out financially, very few are willing to give of their most valuable resource – time. Volunteers are in short supply – constantly. What would you like to do if you had 24 hours a day at your disposal? Would you volunteer to work in a charity shop or would you sign up for a mission to less fortunate areas of the world that are blighted by climate, war and disease? Maybe you would like to work closer to home and help out your local community or perhaps you would like to work with children during breaks from school? Is there a cause that moves you emotionally when you read about it or see the news? Remember, one person can make a difference – you only need to think about the number of lives touched by the love of Mother Teresa or transformed by the vision of Gandhi to know that every one of us can leave a legacy if we so choose.

Other Legacies

According to the English dictionary on my shelf, a legacy is 'something handed down or received from an ancestor or predecessor'.[1] So I guess my last question to you in this section is: 'What are you planning to hand down?' Most of this life area has been concerned with monetary legacies but there is a whole host of other legacies you could leave behind. You may need to begin acquiring or creating them now; for example, will you leave behind items of sentimental value, photographs, letters or handmade craft items? Are you planning to pass on skills and expertise? Is your life worth recording in memoirs? Do you need a biographer or could you write it yourself? All of these are things that will outlive you and should be included in this area of your Life Map.

Creating a Life Map

Now we get to the exciting part of this chapter – creating your Life Map. The technique we are going to use is called mind-mapping. This technique for tapping into the brain's immense power was pioneered by Tony Buzan. Tony realized that the brain requires stimuli on a number of levels if it is to be

---

[1] Collins English Dictionary – Third Edition.

forced either to 'give up' information that is locked away in its deepest vaults or to process information that is acquired throughout the course of the day. Indeed, originally, mind maps were used by individuals seeking to retain great piles of information (particularly useful at exam time), and they are still used today to extraordinary effect by the world's leading memory practitioners.

For our purposes, we are going to use mind map technology to help you release all your hidden dreams and desires. Typically, we are conditioned to lock away our real dreams to avoid ridicule and disappointment. However, for this exercise it is essential that you just let everything flood out onto the paper. Later, when we go through the process of prioritization, you will have the opportunity to sneak a few of them back (for a while at least).

Mind maps are created from words, pictures and colour and only one rule – there are no rules. The way they work is to allow your mind to relax and create links between one piece of information and the next. For example, if you write the word 'travel', that may stimulate you to think of 'flights, tours, cruises, backpacking, package holidays, trains, planes and cars. From the word 'holidays', you might think of a list of countries and destinations that appeal to you; and different countries might inspire a list of activities that you would like to do, such as scuba-diving, bungee jumping or white water rafting. The travel example overleaf should make this process clear.

Grab a piece of paper, some coloured pens and find somewhere quiet where you can relax and think. . . . Okay, are you ready? Good, let's start your amazing journey.

1. Write 'My Life' in the centre of the page and draw a box around it. (From here on, everything you think about will be 'outside the box'.)

2. Draw four short lines, originating from the corners of this box and at the ends of them write the headings Live, Love, Learn and Leave a Legacy.

3. Choose words from the table below to start the process of building your Life Map. This is *your* Life Map, so subtract and add to the lists at your leisure.

4. Make your list as inclusive as possible, leaving nothing in your head.

You may decide to do this exercise with your partner – if you do, please ensure that your individual items are captured as well as your joint items.

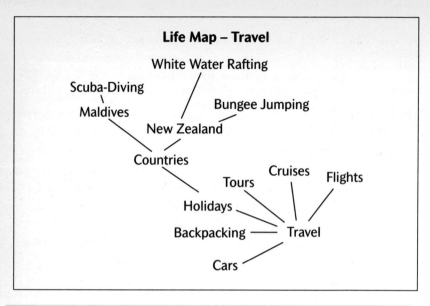

Life Map – some suggested categories

Live	Love	Learn	Leave a Legacy
Travel	Partner	Books	Income
Accommodation	Family	Tapes	Memoirs
Things	Friends	Association	Legacy
Sport		Skills	Charity
Entertainment		Training events	
Health			

As mentioned before, many categories can be relevant in more than one life area of your map. For example, 'holidays' could fit easily into 'Live', 'Love' and 'Learn' if that location was somewhere like Italy – you'd like to see the beautiful Amalfi coastline, you'd love to walk around the romantic piazzas of Venice with your partner and you cannot think of a better way to learn about ancient Roman culture than to walk around the ruins of the Coliseum. The key is to keep writing and try not to focus too much on where individual categories fit. Your brain will determine the best position to ensure that additional and related information is accessed readily.

The example opposite shows you what a Life Map covering all four life areas might look like.

Life Map

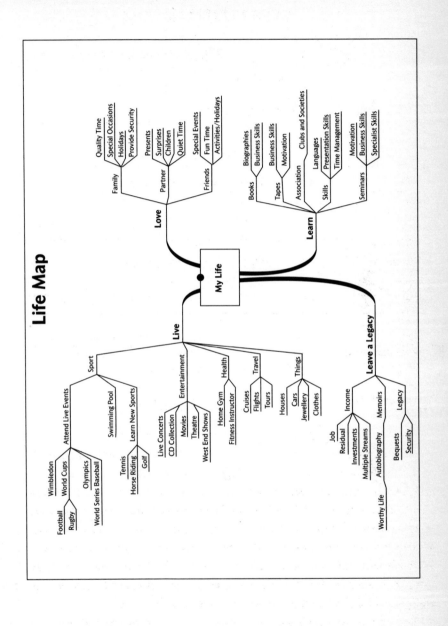

KEY POINTS

- ⤙ A balanced life is one that pays attention to all four life areas – Live, Love, Learn and Leave a Legacy
- ⤙ Your personal balance is derived from an honest appraisal of what you would like to do, have and become in each life area
- ⤙ Review your Life Map regularly; your choices will change as your life develops.

With the foundations in place, it is time to begin creating the framework of our 'time management tower'. It is your goals that bind the structure, and without them your efforts will be wasted. More than anything else, your goals provide you with the all-important 'why' and motivate you to achieve and significantly increase your time management effectiveness – as we'll see in the next chapter.

3 Life goals and goals for life

Your Goal, if you ain't got a Goal, is to get a Goal.

Even the greatest sportsmen cannot score if the target is not constructed. You need goals – otherwise there is no point in becoming better at managing your time. Without goals you are saying to everyone else in your world that you are constantly available to fulfil any demands they may have or ever think of having. However, having completed your Life Map, you have all the ammunition you need to start the lifelong process of goal setting. All you need to do is to convert some of the items on your Life Map into goals. After all, a goal is little more than a dream with a date on it. Before we do that though, let's take a trip to the CAR WASH.

CAR WASH

I woke up this morning inspired to complete the first draft of this chapter on goals. Considering I have not even written more than two sentences already this is no small task. However, in achieving this objective I hope to be able to illustrate the simple process for pursuing a goal that I have followed for a number of years now. It also allows me to introduce goal setting in a very real way. In essence, this goal has all the components of a good goal; it is a CAR WASH goal:

- Chunked
- Ask
- Reviewed
- Written

- Accountable
- Scheduled
- Honest

I haven't made this up just to be different from all the standard texts on goals – there are some real fundamental differences in this process that will help you achieve more of your goals. Let's look at each component of the CAR WASH:

Chunked

My first job for Accenture was as part of a team designing and developing some training for a major utility company in the UK. As part of my induction into the role I was given an overview of what the team was looking to achieve over the course of the next 12 months. It was extremely daunting; we had to train several thousand staff how to use a new computer system that had not even been built yet! Looking around at the team, I suddenly felt overwhelmed. How could a team of just five people achieve the goal?

It was at this point that I was introduced to 'chunking'. Indeed, chunking is one of the main reasons why Accenture is so successful today. Every component activity of the job was identified and drawn up on a project plan. Then each activity was further broken down into smaller and smaller tasks until each of us had a clear list of responsibilities for that week. It was amazing; everything suddenly seemed more achievable. I felt more at ease with my role and the whole team had a sense of purpose.

Chunking is nothing more than breaking down a goal into 'bite-sized' pieces. It is critical that you don't bite off more than you can chew with any one chunk but we'll talk more about that later. One thing you will notice about the chunking process, though, is that you must start with a clear image of the final goal. To use a chocolate analogy, you know how big the bar of chocolate is before you start breaking it into bite-sized pieces. On our training project we knew the size of the overall goal and the specific objectives of the project as a whole.

Before we look at how I have chunked this chapter, let's consider the benefits of chunking:

1. The goal appears more achievable, spurring you on to get started.

2. The first step is obvious.

3. Potential complications can be identified in advance and planned around.

4. Appropriate effort can be allocated at the right time.

5. If more than one person is involved in the achievement of the goal, responsibilities can be identified clearly.

6. Gaps in effort can be planned (allowing for holidays, competing goals and delivery of other inputs or dependencies).

7. Unplanned setbacks can be assessed and the chunks rescheduled quickly.

8. Chunks not completed as planned can give advance warning of potential changes to the overall timeframe for the goal.

9. Lessons learned along the way through 'chunk reviews' may alter the overall goal completely.

This last point is extremely important. You may have heard the saying: 'Set your goals in concrete and your plans in sand.' The main problem I have with this is that it is too inflexible. None of us are imbued with perfect knowledge and it is therefore impossible to predict our needs several months in advance (let alone years). Many goals are medium to long term and, by their nature, they are an assessment of our future requirements based upon today's reality. I have seen many people continuing to strive for their original goals, only to find that they no longer meet the specified objectives when they get there. Be flexible, review constantly and reset goals where necessary. It is important only that you have goals not that you hit every one on time and in budget.

Okay, so let's look at how I chunked my goal of completing this chapter today.

1. Understand the overall goal completely:

   a. Complete my chapter on goals.

   b. Write between 3500 and 4500 words.

   c. Explain the process.

   d. Provide motivation.

   e. Include examples.

2. Break down the goal into bite-sized chunks:

   a. CAR WASH

   b. Goal Maps

3. Schedule reviews (i.e. reread to ensure it makes sense)

   a. After each chunk

4. Anticipate interruptions

   a. Meals

   b. Family time

Well, it's now 11:30 a.m. so I'd better press on with the next stage of the CAR WASH.

ASK

I heard a phrase the other day on a sports programme that made an immediate impression on me – specifically as it relates to goal setting. The commentator was assessing the chances of the English cricket team beating the opposition. He said, 'It's a big ask, but I feel that they can do it.' Brilliant. In one sentence, he managed to summarize the mission ahead of the team. It was not going to be easy, indeed it was going to ask each and every one of them to go beyond their previous achievements. However, he felt they were up to it.

For a goal to motivate you sufficiently, it needs to be a 'big ask'. Goals that are too easy to hit seldom keep the goal setter focused enough to complete the task in hand. It is a bit like the story of the hare and the tortoise. For the hare, winning the race was a foregone conclusion and for the tortoise it was a monumentally huge 'ask'. As we all know, the hare ran off and soon disappeared over the horizon, only to stop and have a snooze when the goal was in sight. Meanwhile, the tortoise approached the race one step at a time (chunking in action) and won the race.

How big are your goals? Can you achieve them with very little effort? Do they keep you awake at night trying to think up new and better ways of achieving them? If not, perhaps you should take five minutes, review some of your most important goals and see how you can make them more challenging.

I did not need to set myself the goal of writing this whole chapter in one day, but I knew it would be a 'big ask' that would inspire me to be more focused than I have been on previous days when I have asked less of myself. On average, I have written about 2000 words per day. Today, I aim to almost double my output. Already I have noticed an improvement in many areas:

- My focus is sharper.
- I am not wasting time worrying over minor details (they can be dealt with later).
- My mind is racing ahead, allowing me to play catch-up with my fingers on the keyboard.
- Ideas and inspiration are coming out of nowhere to make the writing task easier.
- I am having more fun, knowing that I have a specific goal to achieve.

Reviewed

The key to getting good at goal setting and overcoming the tendency to underestimate the time required to complete tasks is the act of reviewing. By constantly asking yourself good questions you can improve your overall performance dramatically over time. Reviewing, as a general time management tool, is essential and we shall return later in the book to look at the specifics of reviewing your overall performance. In a goal setting context, there are three stages to reviewing:

1. Foresight:
   a. Is the goal really achievable?
   b. What will be the challenges?
   c. Do you have all the resources you need to achieve the goal?
   d. If not, can you obtain them or overcome the challenge in time?

2. Insight:
   a. How are things going?
   b. Are there any unforeseen challenges?
   c. Have the plans changed?
   d. Do you need to reset the goal?

3. Hindsight:

    a. How did you do?

    b. What changes would you make to improve the process next time?

    c. Were your timescales realistic?

    d. What occurred that was unanticipated and could you have avoided it?

Review constantly until you get a feel for your personal strengths and weaknesses. Improvements will be gradual at first, but stick with it and keep striving to get better. Here are the answers to my latest 'insight review' for the goal of writing this chapter:

1. How are things going? *Excellently.*

2. Are there any unforeseen challenges? *I have received a few more phone calls than expected relating to our new website, but generally, these have been handled quickly.*

3. Have the plans changed? *Nope.*

4. Do you need to reset the goal? *No, I stick by my original goal of completing this chapter before the end of the day.*

Written

The power of a written goal is mysterious. Writing down your goals, making a commitment on paper, or digitally, seems to bring life to a goal. I have read numerous books that relate the story of the 5 per cent of Harvard students with clear written goals who went on to earn more than the remaining 95 per cent without written goals put together. However, for me, even without this example, the process of writing down each of my goals has always seemed logical for four reasons:

1. It becomes more specific and meaningful.

2. You can start to break it down (chunking).

3. You are focused on 'doing' rather than 'thinking'.

4. An effective goal needs to be understood clearly, and I don't have the best memory in the world, so I need to write it down if I am to review it properly later.

Nevertheless, I understand that there are many of you who will be reading this section, registering the points I am making and still not writing down your goals. Why is that? I can only imagine that this is for one of the following reasons:

1. Fear of failure.
2. You don't believe that this applies to you – it's all in your head.
3. You've had written goals before and you did not achieve them.
4. Your goals do not mean much to you anyway – they are more of a wish list than anything else.

I'll tackle these one at a time to see if we can present you with some new perspectives.

Fear of failure

Let me ask you, what happens if you miss a goal?

- You will still have moved closer to the achievement of your stated aim.
- You will have learned some things.
- You will have joined the group of people who do not achieve every goal they set – and that's all of us.

It doesn't apply to you because your goals are all in your head

This is a tricky one because you are acknowledging that goal setting is the right thing to do, and at the same time, for whatever reason, you are refusing to implement the process that will help you achieve your goals. It is a bit like a verbal agreement between an unscrupulous car dealer and a naive first-time buyer – not worth the paper it's written on. You see, the real problems with storing all your goals in your head are:

- No one else can help you with them.
- You need a great memory.
- Reviewing activities is exceedingly difficult.
- For some mystical reason, you are less likely to achieve your goals than your opponents in the game of life.

However, and this is where I am going to be a little controversial, if you find that you *are* able to keep track of your goals and achieve them at a level to which you are (honestly) content, keep doing what you are doing. But, please, please, please, take some time to write to me and let me know how you do it because I have never heard anyone who has achieved a significant goal say that the whole thing was just stored in his or her head and that it stayed there until it was achieved.

You've had written goals before and you did not achieve them

As I pointed out earlier, if this is your experience, then join the club. I don't know anyone who has achieved every goal they have ever set. In fact, I do not know many people who have achieved *any* goal that they have set first time. Nevertheless, it is important that you are not tempted to throw out the baby with the bath water. Just because the end result was not the one you antici-pated does not mean that the whole process is flawed. It could have been that some of the steps along the way were overlooked or you were not aware of all the outside factors affecting your goal. Perhaps the reviews were not com-prehensive enough to identify potential challenges before the goal was in sight? Maybe the timeframes were unrealistic given the scale of the challenge? Possibly you did not have access to a mentor who could have steered you in the right direction if you were going off-track? Who knows? The important thing is to keep trying, review your previous attempts and learn from them.

Your goals do not mean much to you anyway – they are more of a wish list than anything else

I refuse to believe that anyone reading this book could feel that this is true of him or her. You have already indicated your desire to acquire some new skills by picking this book and reading this far. You may not have much confidence in your own ability to achieve your goals right now, but let me assure you that if you don't set yourself goals, you will miss out on achieving any of them entirely, so what have you got to lose?

Accountable

When we were discussing the need to write down your goals, I mentioned that one benefit of doing this was that other people could help you if they know what goals you have. Accountability means taking this one step further and inviting someone else, or even a group of other people, to actively assist you stay on track and do what you said you would do. At this point your goal needs to be measurable or your assistants will be unable to help you.

There are occasions when you can hold yourself accountable and writing this chapter is one such occasion for me. The secret is to obtain as much 'leverage' on yourself as possible. By this, I mean you need to create enough reasons to make you want to achieve your goal so that failure to do so is not an option. Again, in my case, I have told everyone reading this chapter that my goal is to complete it today and while I could lie and say that I did it even if I did not, integrity is important enough to me to provide all the leverage I need to keep myself to my stated goal.

When you are accountable to someone else, though, you can call on all sorts of additional forces to assist you in your mission.

- Fear of failure – in this context, if your fear of letting down someone else is greater than your willingness to let your goal slip away, you're on to a winner.
- Integrity – doing what you said you would do is a strong motivator for many people.
- Being a team player – wherever possible aim to make your goal part of a team goal so that when you are running out of energy, you've got a whole bunch of people urging you forward.
- Recognition – many people are motivated by the possibility of being recognized for their achievements.

An important decision in your quest for accountability is to choose an appropriate mentor or coach. Your mentor should believe first in you and secondly in your ability to achieve your goals. One health warning in relation to identifying a mentor is to be sure to choose someone who also believes in your goals. Their motivation for the completion of your goals needs to be almost as high as yours if they are to keep you to the task. Finally, make sure that your mentor is not afraid to tell you what you *need* to hear rather than what you would *like* to hear!

Scheduled

This one is obvious – which is why it gets overlooked so often. At the very start of this chapter, I said that a goal is nothing more than a dream with a date on it. Well, here's where you get to put a date on your dreams.

Let me start by acknowledging that you may feel a little anxious committing to dates that are too far in the future to feel comfortable. That's okay; the Goal Map we will create at the end of this chapter will help you overcome this anxiety. Beyond that, all I can say is that this is no more uncomfortable than any other task you undertake for the first time – it will become more comfortable with time and practice.

The act of scheduling adds a further dimension to your goals, for the brain registers the commitment to a date in such a way that, once the subconscious has taken hold, it begins to work out other ways of completing the tasks involved.

Of course, setting a deadline also creates additional energy by focusing your efforts, especially as the deadline becomes ever closer – it is human nature to increase effort as a deadline looms. For those who struggle with time management or are constantly interrupted, a deadline produces the necessary levels of adrenalin to help complete the task in time. For successful time managers, a deadline still increases energy levels and allows them to increase the quality of their outputs.

In my example, the deadline to complete this chapter today is extremely specific and has certainly raised the energy level at my desk. Currently, I am running behind schedule and I may need to review my plans – but I can do that because, as you have seen, so far my goal has been put through most of the CAR WAS . . .

Honesty

Well, here we are at the final stage of our goal setting CAR WASH. You may think that honesty is a funny word to be using in the context of an important business skill such as goal setting and you would be right. However, this is no ordinary business book and I don't want you to treat it as such. Many business books get filed on the bookshelf and forgotten as if their usefulness was limited to one scan. By now I hope you will have gathered that the aim of this book is to be more useful than that. This final step in goal setting is the one that changes the activity from a useful business skill into an essential life skill.

Those of you who have read other time management books may recognize some of what I am about to tell you. In particular, you may know that the 'R' of the SMART management acronym represents the word realistic. The claim is that your goals should be realistic. However, I am not convinced. Many people hide behind this word when the reality is that they are too lazy to set goals and strive to achieve them. Some give up before they have reached their goal and many before they even start. You will have heard these people saying things like: 'I understand all the benefits that this would give me, but realistically I haven't got time', 'Realistically, I don't think anyone would be interested at that price' or 'I'm just being realistic – it's not worth the effort'.

The frustrating thing is that the people who say these things sound so genuine, rational and above all else incredibly *reasonable*. Indeed, these people rationalize very well but, as a good friend of mine says, that just means that they are good at telling 'rational lies'.

> The reasonable man adapts himself to the world; the unreasonable one persists in trying to adapt the world to himself. Therefore all progress depends on the unreasonable man.
>
> George Bernard Shaw

Don't try to be realistic because the reality is you do not have all the facts. If something is worthwhile, do it. If something is not working, evaluate what you are doing – honestly. Are you doing everything according to the best experience in that particular field? Are you applying all of the advice your mentor is giving or are you listening selectively and only doing those things with which you are most comfortable? Do not make decisions based purely on previous experience – just look at all the things that could have changed since then:

- Your attitude
- Your circumstances
- Your income
- Your security
- Your family
- Your motivation
- Your outlook
- The economy

- Trends and fashion
- The market
- Morality and values

Do you see why it may be 'realistic' to make a particular judgement or decision, but it is not necessarily 'honest'?

On a micro goal setting level, honesty will help you steer clear of the pitfalls of thinking that something is impossible. When you review your efforts, do so honestly; you are fooling yourself if you fabricate reasons for lack of achievement in any area. Of course, the great thing about goals, which you now know, is that very few people achieve them straight away. So, go easy on yourself and allow mistakes and errors of judgement and even stupidity on occasion. It is all a process of learning and, once you have grasped the basics, nothing will stop you. This is why so many millionaires have made and lost fortunes repeatedly. Each loss was an honest learning point, each gain the result of wisdom and a determination to do better.

So, the question is not 'Is this goal attainable?' The question should be 'Is this goal worth my time and effort?' If you answer that positively you can be sure that you will find ways to make it happen and if it does not happen the first time by the specified deadline, try again.

Goal Maps

The shortest distance between any two points can be determined only when you know where those two points are. Another blindingly obvious statement, you may say. However, it is amazing how many people walk around in life not knowing where they want to go. The result is any route will take them there because 'there' has not been defined. If you have taken the time to define where you want to go next, then this activity will be very simple.

Goal Maps are a graphical way of representing your main goals and charting out the route to get you there. The key is to start with two or three of your goals on the right-hand side of the page and then trace a route *backwards* until you arrive at the first steps you need to take on the way to achieving your goals. First, though, you need to make your goals incredibly specific. Vague goals, such as 'I'd like to earn more money' or 'I'd like to be in better shape' will not work. Get specific. So if you want to earn more, state the exact amount and pick a date when you will be earning that amount. If you want to be in better shape, write down the body measurements you are aiming for, the ideal weight you would like to be and some fitness measures that your fitness instructor can help you generate.

When I look at a completed Goal Map it seems to be so obvious as to be insulting, but I can assure you that is not the intention. This 'left to right' perspective can look simple – for example, it makes complete sense that in order to read Shakespeare's works you will need to purchase them first. However, it is usually the first steps that are the most difficult to anticipate when you set yourself a big goal. Many delegates on our courses have found this exercise incredibly beneficial, as it has led them to some first steps that they had not previously considered. The aim is to make the first steps as simple as possible to provide you with the momentum to go on to the next step, and the next, until the goal is achieved.

The example below shows you what a Goal Map might look like.

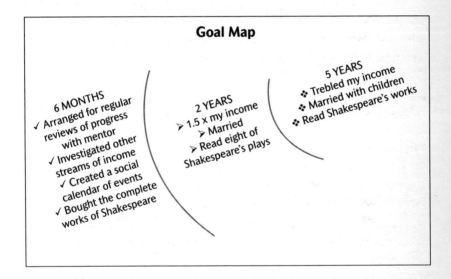

Goal Map

6 MONTHS
✓ Arranged for regular reviews of progress with mentor
✓ Investigated other streams of income
✓ Created a social calendar of events
✓ Bought the complete works of Shakespeare

2 YEARS
➢ 1.5 x my income
➢ Married
➢ Read eight of Shakespeare's plays

5 YEARS
❖ Trebled my income
❖ Married with children
❖ Read Shakespeare's works

The real value of Goal Maps, though, is in the review stages, which are shown in the next Goal Map, overleaf. Logical progression through your tasks should lead you directly to your goal (Route A). However, if you find yourself going slightly off-track it is a simple task for you and your mentor to devise a programme to get you back in line before the timeframe for the next stage (Stage 2 in our example) has elapsed (Route B). If left unchecked, a small diversion in Stage 1 of your plan can lead to you missing your goals by a long way (Route C).

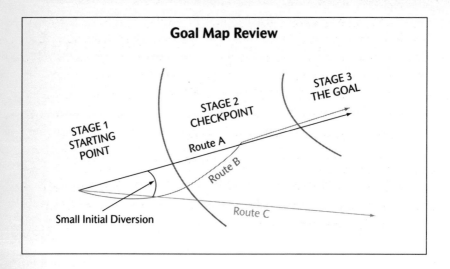

Goal Map Review

STAGE 3
THE GOAL

STAGE 2
CHECKPOINT

STAGE 1
STARTING
POINT

Route A

Route B

Small Initial Diversion

Route C

ACTIVITY

Why not take some of the items from your Life Map and place them into a Goal Map of your own? Set your own timescales and work backwards until you identify some simple, clear first steps that will get you moving towards your dreams.

So that's the end of the chapter on goals, and I guess many of you will be wondering how I have done against mine. Well, if I tell you that it is now 11:25 p.m., you will see that I have done it. It also brings me to another point about goals – they can drive you to all sorts of effort at strange times of the day. Normally, I would have finished writing hours ago, but I didn't want to miss my goal. Hope you find it useful.

KEY POINTS

↳ Goals are essential to living your life and managing your time effectively.

⊷ Your goals may change over time, but just be sure to put them through the CAR WASH:

- Chunk them into bite-sized pieces.

- Ask a lot of yourself, it's the only way you will find out your true potential.

- Review them frequently to stay on track.

- Write them down.

- Accountability will ensure your success.

- Scheduling completion will keep you focused

- Honesty is the most valuable self-help tool available.

⊷ Your Goal Map is an interactive, fluid tool – use it often to review, change and refocus your efforts.

Okay, why don't we start building our 'time management tower' in earnest – secure in the knowledge that the foundations and supporting beams are in place?

4 An introduction to Time Styles[1]

Something has always bothered me about traditional approaches to time management – the insistence on trying to make everyone feel that they should conform to some 'normal' way of doing things. Who says planning before you go to sleep or first thing in the morning is normal anyway? Surely it does not matter when you plan or, indeed, do any of the other key time management activities, as long as you do it? What is important is to utilize your own strengths and weaknesses to create a personalized approach to life management.

The first place to start is with you – what is your Time Style? How do you view the whole issue of time management? Is it something that comes naturally to you, or are you struggling to get from one over-running meeting to another half-forgotten appointment?

My perspective on this issue was revolutionized a couple of years ago when I heard Dr Robert Rohm speak on personality styles at a conference I attended. Like all good teachers, he used humour liberally and was able to impart his key messages in one short session. In his presentation he outlined four broad 'types' of people and their typical approaches to life's challenges. I loved it. For the first time, I heard someone explain how to understand yourself and those around you better. Using a very simple model – the DISC model – he created four distinct profiles that accounted for everyone that I knew. For those of you familiar with Dr Rohm's work,[2] you can broadly

---

[1] Copyright Simesco Limited.
[2] Dr Robert Rohm, *Positive Personality Profiles*. Personality Insights Inc., First Edition, 1992.

equate his DISC model with our TIME model described below (i.e. D = T, I = I, S = M, C = E). All I have done is look at the particular issues and challenges around time management and personal development through the perspective of the DISC model and utilized different letters to highlight my specific points. Dr Rohm's model itself has quite a history and many of you will relate some components of the model back to the hypocratic temperaments made most famous by William Shakespeare: choleric; sanguine; phlegmatic; and melancholic.

The two questions you need to ask yourself to determine your Time Style are:

1. Are you 'outgoing' or 'reserved'?

2. Are you more 'task' or 'people' focused?

Your answers to those questions will result in a placement somewhere in the diagram below:

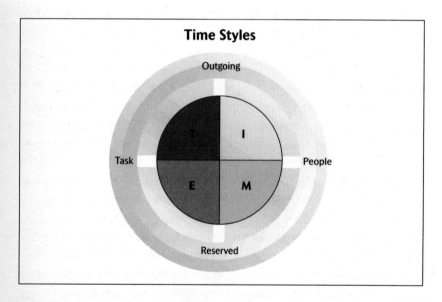

Time Styles

It is possible that you may fall somewhere between two options (being equally task and people focused, for example). If this is the case, ask your closest friend or colleague, or your partner, which behaviour you demonstrate most often. For the purposes of this exercise, go with your tendency – you can always change your mind later.

You may be wondering why an understanding of your Time Style is important in the context of time management, so let's look at a straightforward transaction, the purchase of a handheld computer. You may recognize some of the characteristics displayed by our four shoppers.

Mrs T takes immediate action. She goes to the up-market department store during the lunch hour, identifies three possible options, quickly narrows down the choice and then asks for a good discount – after all, if she likes the device, she could refer a lot of good clients to the shop. Satisfied that she has made the right choice, Mrs T returns to work and delegates the task of setting up the handheld to her secretary.

Dr I wants the best handheld on the market. He has seen several models in his favourite magazine that look great, but he hasn't had time to wade through all of the technical information. On arrival at the gadget shop, he asks the sales assistant for a look at the coolest handhelds they have. Sensing an ideal 'up-selling' opportunity, the assistant brings back just two examples: one that is relatively cheap but functional, the other the most expensive, exclusive, extraordinary handheld in stock. Dr I doesn't really listen to the sales assistant's patter but instead inserts comments of his own, such as 'this colour is really cool' and 'that one will fit in my jacket pocket'. Of course, he buys the more expensive model, especially when the assistant shows him all the games that can be played on it. When he gets home, Dr I puts the instruction booklet to one side and spends the next half hour trying to understand how it all works. Having worked out some of the basic elements, he gets bored and sets about achieving some high scores on his new 'games unit'.

Miss M is not sure that she needs an electronic organizer. She's been doing okay for years with the 'Lifofax' her father brought home from work for her to use. It's true that she spends hours each year updating her names and addresses, but the whole exercise is quite cathartic really. It is only when her brother suggests that she should 'join the rest of us in the twenty-first century' that she finally decides to investigate the options. She spends a long time looking through the magazines to see which models are the most popular (this is usually a good way of assessing the best purchase to make). Nevertheless, she is still undecided when she gets to the shop. With just two options remaining after 20 minutes she asks the assistant which one he would buy. Before leaving with her new handheld, though, she checks the returns policy – it would be dreadful to have made the wrong decision and not have the opportunity to change her mind later. Once she has transferred all her data from her diary and address books into her handheld, she begins to worry whether her friends will think she is being 'flash' with her new gadget.

Prof. E writes down a whole list of questions that he needs addressed before he will make his purchase. A thorough search of the Internet (aided by a spreadsheet of criteria) reveals two models that are clearly ahead on functionality and price. Determining that there are possibly four local stores that sell both of these models, he plans his journey around these stores carefully. In each store, he presents his list of criteria and asks a further set of questions concerning price and availability, documenting the answers in his notebook. After visiting the stores, he goes to the coffee shop to look at the relative benefits of each offer before returning to his chosen store and making his purchase. Confident that he has made the correct choice he returns home to begin the process of setting up his new handheld. He is very glad that he took a whole day off work to get this important job done.

Now I understand that I have employed an element of poetic licence (and plain exaggeration) to illustrate the style differences; but I hope this has helped you to begin to identify how your approach can be coloured quite significantly by your style. The purpose of this chapter is to look at how understanding your own Time Style can help you become a better time manager. Also, by understanding and working with the Time Styles of the people around you, you will be able to achieve more and help others get what they want too.

Understanding your Time Style

T – Outgoing and Task Focused

If your Time Style is 'T', you are likely to be quite demanding (of yourself and others). Once you have fixed your mind on a goal, you are extremely tenacious. You are unrelenting in your activity until the job is done. You use phrases like 'You can take it to the bank', 'My word is my bond' and 'It's my way or the highway!'. Although you are task focused, your outgoing nature can deceive others who may interpret your behaviour wrongly as being more like an 'I'. The real you will shine through, though, when

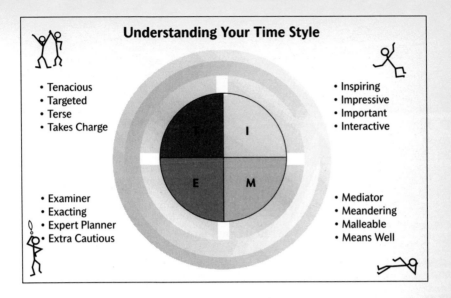

Understanding Your Time Style

- Tenacious
- Targeted
- Terse
- Takes Charge

- Inspiring
- Impressive
- Important
- Interactive

- Examiner
- Exacting
- Expert Planner
- Extra Cautious

- Mediator
- Meandering
- Malleable
- Means Well

T I

E M

your goal is in sight – nothing and (more importantly) no one gets in your way.

In terms of time management fundamentals, your favourite tool is the 'To Do' list. Nothing gives you greater pleasure than to put a huge tick against each item on your list as you complete it. Being action oriented, the creation of a list, before getting started, just seems like common sense to you. In addition, it gives you a sense of control over your time so that 'other people' can't get in the way of you achieving what you want to do today.

In one respect, the whole task of time management appeals to your sense of order and control. Activities such as long- and short-term goal setting are almost second nature to you. Where things start to go astray are in areas where the achievement of the goal involves interaction with others. Indeed, the main thing you need to watch out for is your propensity to be quite terse when you are dealing with people. In your eagerness to get the job done, you can sometimes ignore the feelings of those around you. Not that this bothers you normally. If other people cannot understand your motivation – that's their problem.

I – Outgoing and People Focused

If you are an 'I' person, I would just like to say 'thank you' for sticking with it. I don't mean that in a patronizing way. Many I's will know what I mean when I say that concentration is not one of your strong points. Unless, of course, the activity requiring your concentration is a whole lot of fun. Typically, you love to make a grand entrance. You are very concerned by the opinions that others have of you and would like to think that you are important. Sometimes this need for external approval can hold you back from attempting things that you would like to try because you are afraid of the impression it will give others.

Your general approach to time management is haphazard – and that is being kind. You can often be heard using phrases like 'Don't worry, it's all in my head', 'Am I late? Never mind, I'm here now, let the party begin' and 'Count me in. Where did you say we were going?'.

It's not that you intend to be forgetful; it's just that when plans are being made or deadlines are being agreed, you are usually distracted by something equally important and usually more urgent. Indeed, most of your life is spent running from one over-run meeting to the next almost forgotten appointment. We will return later to discuss some strategies that you can employ to improve your time management; but, for now, spend some time considering how much more 'fun' you could have if you could just streamline all of the administration in your life and get it done more efficiently.

M – Reserved and People Focused

While the T's hustle and bustle and the I's amuse and entertain us, the M's can usually be found in the background labouring away tirelessly, getting everything done so that the rest of us can just enjoy ourselves. It is almost as if M's are running on long life batteries. Your prime interest in life is to 'get through it'. If you can do this with minimum fuss and maximum harmony, you are extremely grateful.

Many people misinterpret your accommodating nature and assume you are a 'pushover' – this is their first and, quite often, their last mistake. When M's feel that they have been wronged or, more importantly, that their loved ones have been wronged, you can be sure that you will know about it – maybe not straight away but in ways that will demonstrate clearly your mistake.

Nevertheless, herein lies the real challenge for M's in the area of time management. As you are so innately nice, you will try to accommodate everyone else and forget about your own needs. However, in trying to accommodate everyone, you typically manage to please no one because your efforts are spread so thinly.

In reality, of course, every team needs an M if they are to finish the job that the excited I's started and keep everyone happy in the process. In short, M's are the oil that makes the engine run smoothly.

E – Reserved and Task Focused

The 'E' types invented time management – of that, there can be no doubt. E's are always creating systems out of chaos; it is the way they are constructed. In fact, when we were devising this book and thinking about its appeal to the four Time Styles, we ranked them in the following order:

1. E's – to file alongside their existing time management collection.

2. T's – attracted by the opportunity to master another skill.

3. M's – always open to the possibility to improve.

4. I's – the book is not too big and has some cool pictures in it.

Of course, within a few minutes, you E's will have ascertained a potential percentage breakdown of these four groups and maybe even thought through seven ways that we could have boosted sales further with a structured and individualized marketing strategy.

By the way, if you have read this far and have not been able to decide which Time Style you are, why not be an E for the purposes of this chapter? You can always change your mind once you have examined all of the evidence. Allow for a margin of error of, say, 9.6%.

Your main challenge as an E, in a time management context, is to force yourself to act upon all of the knowledge that you have acquired. The decision making process is exactly that – a process, not a result.

Your main assets are your attention to detail, your capacity to remember all sorts of useful information and your ability to dissect, analyse and interpret even the most complex problems. The world needs geniuses like you.

Sounds Like a Good Excuse to Me!

The reason for identifying the four different Time Styles was not to give you an excuse for your current poor time management. Everyone, even the most extreme I can take control of their lives and become better at managing their time – if that is their choice. The purpose of the Time Style model is to provide a useful insight into the main challenges you will face when learning to implement some of the strategies outlined in this book. In addition, having an understanding of the Time Styles of others will improve your interaction with them and further enhance your own time management.

A motive for action

Every one of us – and each Time Style – will have a different motive for wanting to improve our time management. However, there is one common factor that all of us must recognize – there are only 24 hours in a day (denoted by the clock face in the Time Style diagrams). The most simple incentive to get better at managing your time is the fact that it creates more opportunity to do the things you want to do as well as ensuring that there is enough time to do the things you must.

In Chapter 2, you developed a Life Map to clarify some of your specific

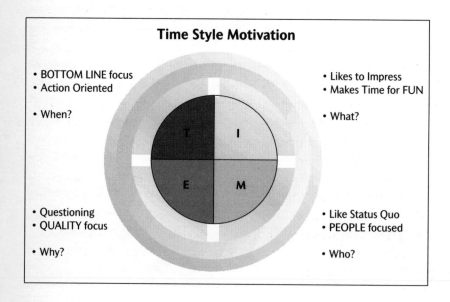

Time Style Motivation

- BOTTOM LINE focus
- Action Oriented

- When?

- Likes to Impress
- Makes Time for FUN

- What?

- Questioning
- QUALITY focus

- Why?

- Like Status Quo
- PEOPLE focused

- Who?

motives for action. Now, let's look at some of the typical motivators for your specific Time Style.

T – What's the Bottom Line?

The bottom line result of getting better at time management is that you will have more time to achieve the list of goals you have set your heart on. T's love a challenge and enjoy all the success and acclaim that they earn along the way. Whoever said 'It is not the winning that counts, but the taking part' was obviously not a T. For a T, winning is everything; winning is not negotiable.

The good news is that when you improve your time management skills, you will improve the bottom line in all areas of your life and dramatically increase your chances of winning in the game of life. That is not to say that being a good time manager is a magic cure – you will not become a better person just by being more effective with your time, for example. However, a lot of what we do is measured on results, and having more control of how you allocate your time will release you from the constraints you may experience currently.

I – When Do I Have Time for Fun?

I's hate to miss out on anything, especially if there is fun involved. Frequently, however, in your rush to agree to the multitude of invitations you receive, you double-book and sometimes even triple-book yourself. Now obviously, using a diary will not create the opportunity for you to accept two invitations that are planned for the same time; but how often have you found that when the time is being set in the first place there is room for manoeuvre? If you had access to, and used, a diary, you could anticipate overlaps and make sure your schedule was free of clashes.

Through planning your time in advance, you can save time by grouping similar activities and strategically planning your appointments to minimize organizational and travelling time. We will return later to look at some of the key time saving tips that will help you. For now, it is only important that you understand that improving your time management skills will provide you with more opportunities to do the things you like to do and to be with the people you like to be with.

M – How Can I Help Others Best?

The wise M knows that the real benefits of time management extend beyond the personal payback of control and liberation discussed already. In many respects, M's see time management, and many other activities they conduct, as a mechanism for achieving and doing more, as part of a team or a family. Teamwork, it is said, makes the dream work; and time management can add to your individual effectiveness as part of any team.

In the context of digital time management, a number of the advantages of digital systems over paper-based systems appeal to M's. For example, the ability to capture in the same place the personal details of your friends and colleagues, and attach useful notes such as directions to their house, is priceless to M's. Chapter 11, Advanced digital time-ology, includes many tips that will enhance your reputation for remembering special events, celebrations and occasions.

E – How Will Time Management Improve the Quality of My Life?

E's love gadgets, and, in particular, time-saving devices. You may not be the first to go out and buy the latest models – you leave that to the more impulsive I's and direct T's. However, once you have decided that something is useful and provides good value, you relish the prospect of acquiring your new device.

Handheld computers are good value for money and here are some specific reasons why:

- They can hold more information than you will ever need.
- Access to important information is instant and grouped logically.
- Linked information can be organized and accessed effectively.
- Multiple copies of the information can be maintained to avoid data loss.

In summary, all digital time devices such as handhelds, desktop organizers and web-based calendars are effective time management tools that leave you more time to conduct value added activities.

KEY POINTS

⊢ Effective time management is a matter of style – use your strengths:

- T's are good decision makers and can whip up a task list in no time.
- I's are great enthusiasts and can get any show on the road.
- M's have tireless patience and are excellent team players.
- E's are meticulous and will always finish the job – on time and within budget.

⊢ There is no right way to manage your time – just *your* way.

⊢ Understand your own Time Style so that you can conduct yourself accordingly, enlisting help in areas of personal weakness.

Understanding your Time Style is only the start. Managing yourself is where the fun really starts, and with home working on the increase, time management has never been more important.

5 Manage yourself

Whether you run your business from home, travel around the country completing your tasks out of hotel rooms, work from home a couple of days a week or fly around the world stopping in airport lounges and cyber cafes to conduct your business – you need to know that you can depend on yourself when it comes to getting the job done.

This chapter contains all the tools you need, including some daily habits that reinforce success, a prioritization system that really works and some easy-to-implement methods for overcoming procrastination. Only then will you be equipped to jump into the Results Cyclone and achieve maximum performance.

The challenges of home working

The key challenges associated with working from home or anywhere away from your colleagues revolve around the issue of expectations. The diagram below illustrates the 'attitude curve' that individuals go through as they embark on remote working. The person who starts their own home-based business experiences similar feelings.

Let's consider each significant point on the attitude curve in turn:

1. Decision

   When employees are told that they will be working from home their initial

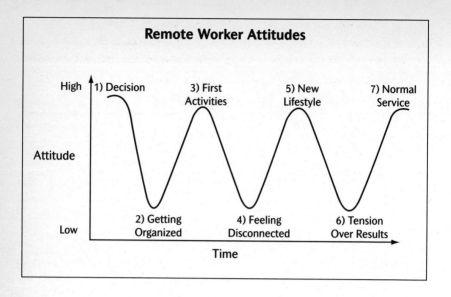

Remote Worker Attitudes

reaction can be one of joy – especially if they are the ones who have been promoting it.

2. Getting organized

   However, they then get embroiled in setting up the office at home and this can bring with it a whole host of challenges, which include the following:

   a. There is little room to get organized.

   b. The office is shared with living space.

   c. Children and partners have to be 'trained' to respect your need for space when working.

   d. Interruptions can come from a whole host of sources: phone calls, deliveries, neighbours, power cuts.

   e. Motivation can be low and distractions such as food and drink and the television too available.

   f. Life and work can become merged.

3. First activities

   Launching yourself into your first activities can be a lot of fun, especially when you realize that working from home can be more productive than working in an office. You can start an hour earlier because you no longer need to commute. Once you have organized your family and tamed the electronic interruptions, you can become extremely focused and get work done in relative peace.

4. Feeling disconnected

The most popular complaint of home workers everywhere is that they no longer feel a sense of community. They miss the camaraderie of the workplace, the banter at the coffee machine, the jokes and the gossip. Sometimes, the need to communicate with another human being is so strong that they will fabricate reasons to call the office or other people in the team. Added to this problem of social isolation is the overall downgrading of technical infrastructure that some people have to contend with once the decision to be based at home has been agreed. Typically, the Internet connections are less robust (causing the email to crash just when you are in the middle of sending a critical document on which you have been working for hours), and unless your company has furnished you with the latest telephone technology, you are left with an inadequate tool for dealing with business interactions.

5. New lifestyle

Just when you think it's time to call a halt to this 'experiment', you are asked to help organize a party for your parents' silver wedding anniversary. Normally, this would have to be done on weekends, in between shopping at the supermarket and fixing the washing machine. However, now you are able to integrate this task into your day and actually get it done twice as quickly because all the people with whom you need to deal are available. In fact, overall, your life is far less stressful than it seemed to be when you were working in the office.

6. Tension over results

This is the most difficult area to deal with initially, but if you persist and work together with your team to crack the nut, the rest of the time you spend working remotely will run very smoothly. It can be challenging being a manager of a team that is working remotely; you would like to trust them, but your mind is constantly questioning the whole situation:

a. Are they working on the job as many hours as they should be?

b. Are they focused?

c. Are they following up the queries that needed further investigation as a result of your last conversation?

d. Are their progress reports truthful?

I think you can see the problem; unfortunately, the only answer that makes sense is for both parties to communicate effectively and to 'trust until'. Only then can remote teams exhibit the same synergy that best performing co-located teams exhibit. Clear communication of expectations, and plenty of process checks early in the assignment of new tasks, is the quickest way to achieve results.

7. Normal service

Once the communication systems are in place and everyone understands the requirements of their team, working remotely becomes a stroll in the park – quite literally.

Daily habits

It takes about 30 days to acquire a habit. 30 days of repeated activity. What follows are some standard time management techniques that will greatly enhance the balance in your life and increase your overall effectiveness significantly. I do not intend to go into lots of detail about these because they are mostly self-explanatory; these are quick-fire, proven ideas for being effective in the 24/7 world.

Pareto's 80/20 Rule

You will get 80 per cent of the work done with only 20 per cent of the total effort required.

This is a heart-warming adaptation of the original analysis because in essence it means that you are going to have a lot to show for your efforts after applying only 20 per cent of the energy required to do the whole job. Of course, as every student will know, this is the principle by which most work gets done. You start a job, apply 20 per cent of the total effort required and still get 80 per cent of the work done – which leaves plenty of time for drinking, partying and having fun.

This technique is especially useful if you are developing something new in a team environment. Your initial 20 per cent effort will produce lots for your teammates to ponder, supplement and modify. Initially, your colleagues will not have fixed ideas on what should be included in the new project, so your first thoughts will also provide the framework for focused thinking.

The Steal 180 Rule

How would you like a technique for obtaining an extra 180 hours a year? Sounds great, doesn't it? Well, here's how you do it: get up half an hour earlier. That's 3.5 hours a week, or nearly 180 hours a year.[1]

I know some of you are reading this and thinking 'I get up early enough already' and that's fine; but let me ask you, could you get up half an hour earlier if it was really important? If you had to get up half an hour earlier to collect your winning lottery prize – could you do it? If the answer is 'Yes' then your excuse has just flown out of the window.

Of course, there is no point in getting up earlier if you are going to waste that extra time watching television or reading the newspaper; but just imagine what you could achieve if you had an extra 180 hours a year (the equivalent of 4.5 average working weeks). You might decide to use your half hour to do that exercise routine you resolved to complete at New Year, or maybe you would read a good book (with half an hour a day you could probably complete 12 good books a year). Whatever it is, why not get up earlier tomorrow and make a start?

Getting Organized

You know what you need to do to get organized. You certainly don't need me to tell you about creating workable systems and routines for your regular activities. However, the reason for putting this under the section on daily habits is to give you some hope if you consider yourself to be disorganized right now. You can become organized and stay organized if you will commit to a 30-day programme and stick to it. Set aside 30 minutes each day and take some small steps towards getting yourself in order. You may find it useful to spend your first 30 minutes drawing up a list of all the little things that you

---

[1] An alternative way of obtaining another 30 minutes would be to watch half an hour less television each day – you choose.

could do on subsequent days, such as setting up direct debits for your regular bills and creating files for each of your current projects. Be strict with your time keeping and don't allow yourself to get carried away with any one organizing activity or you will reinforce your current perception that being organized is an arduous, boring activity that takes a lot of time. Instead, you want to build a new perception that it doesn't take long to get organized and that staying organized is even easier.

Planning For Success

No doubt you will have heard the saying, 'Those who fail to plan, plan to fail'; nothing could be truer. Think of planning as a more detailed version of chunking. All you are doing is setting out your best guess as to what needs to be done next and breaking each task down into its component pieces. For example, you need to prepare dinner tomorrow evening for guests, so your plan could include the following:

1. Shopping list
2. Shopping
3. Preparation
4. Cooking
5. Presentation

More complex plans work from the same principle. Ask good questions:

- What needs to be done and in what order?
- Are there any other things that will have an impact on the plan?
- Who else needs to be involved?
- What potential problems can be anticipated?

It does not need to be any more complicated than this. Keep it simple and plan whenever you can. For best results co-ordinate your planning activities with the reviewing routines that we will discuss in Chapter 9.

ACTIVITY

Start acquiring good time management habits today. Set aside 30 minutes *today* to write a plan for your first steps towards managing yourself more effectively.

Prioritizing made simple

I have read some rubbish on prioritizing. I have even tried to implement a whole range of different techniques for identifying what needs to get done and in what order (indeed, I have taught some of them), but the bottom line is that none of them work. At least, none of them work consistently. I have met people from all walks of life and from many different industries in Europe, the USA and Africa, and when I look at what they actually *do* when prioritizing their work, it is never as complex as the various systems I have been taught or read about in books. The reason is that the prioritizing systems that have been written down invariably are not intuitive. For example, some of you will be familiar with the 2 × 2 model, which has four levels of priority – Sectors 1, 2, 3 and 4 – based on the axes 'urgency' and 'importance'. But can any of you remember whether Sector 2 is 'urgent and not important' or 'not urgent and important'? Recently, I read about a system of prioritization that suggested everything should fall into A, B, C, D or E levels of priority but when I asked a friend to relate the levels to me he could not remember the difference between levels B and C.

Most people that I have observed rarely work with more than three levels of priority and they get tremendous results.

The prioritization method I am going to show you is based upon a system invented by a life coach and very good friend of mine – Nicola Carew.[1] It is brilliant because it is literally as simple as 1, 2, 3. The other good thing about it is that it explains *how* the majority of people who manage their time well actually do it.

1, 2, 3

As you go through the day acquiring items to add to your 'To Do' list wouldn't it be great to prioritize them straight away? Well with the 1, 2, 3 System you can. Similarly, wouldn't it be fantastic if you could rely on your intuition to help you prioritize your tasks rather than needing to think about it? Again, this system can work for you.

The 1, 2, 3 System is precisely that: a system that allows you to prioritize

---

[1] The Management Focus Index – copyright of CWL. For more information contact Nicola Carew – nac@cwl1.demon.co.uk

tasks in only one of three groups. The secret is in the focus of each of the groups:

- Priority 1 – Will contribute directly to the achievement of your goals
- Priority 2 – Will indirectly contribute to your goals
- Priority 3 – Will not affect your goals

I hope that Chapter 3 will have helped you to clarify your goals, so Priorities 1 and 2 should be very clear in your mind. Each day you should work on Priority 1 and 2 tasks until they are finished or your time has run out. Over time your aim is to reduce the amount of time you spend on Priority 3 activities until they are eliminated from your lists, so the key to this system is to understand Priority 3.

Essentially, Priority 3 tasks are those that will not move you towards the achievement of your goals. Critically, though, this does not mean that some of the tasks that end up in this group are unimportant. For example, I have just been offered a ticket to see England play against Sweden in a football match. Watching international sporting events around the globe is on my Life Map, but there are no specific events on my current list of goals and my diary is full for the next week. The only way this will become a real opportunity for me is if some of the activities currently on my Priority 1 and 2 lists get cancelled or postponed.

Another feature of Priority 3 tasks is that they can be delegated to others. This is delegation in the truest sense and for the right reasons. A lot of business activities are delegated for the wrong reasons, usually because the delegator finds the task boring or onerous. However, if a task is not contributing to your current list of goals then delegation is the best option, especially if it is contributing to someone else's goals or perhaps the business goals of your team. In my case, if I am unable to go to the match, I will need to delegate the task to someone who has it on their list of goals and is looking for a ticket – or more likely, someone without goals.

Now I know that some of you will need convincing that this system is comprehensive enough to cope with all of your tasks, so I thought I would answer a few Frequently Asked Questions to illustrate its durability.

How does this method differentiate between work and life tasks?

The method does not – you do! When you were constructing your Goal Map you will have identified a number of goals that were either work related or relationship/life related. By utilizing the 1, 2, 3 System you will no longer differentiate between work and home goals unthinkingly; instead, you will aim to achieve your activities on a daily basis according to their focus on and contribution towards your goals. So, if you have goals in your personal life as well as your work life, they are equally important – you should apply equal priority to them. It is because so many people typically prioritize work over their other life activities and goals that we have so many one-dimensional members of society – neither building good relationships with their families and friends nor contributing meaningfully to their communities. It is pointless setting yourself goals in all areas of your life if you are going to continue 'de-prioritizing' the non-work items on a daily basis.

What if I have two tasks and one is more urgent than the other?

Who cares? What meaningful difference does the notion of urgency make to a specific activity? When you happen across something that is screaming 'Urgent' at you, ask yourself, 'What difference will this make to my life in five years' time if I do not deal with this straight away?' Typically, the answer is, 'Very little'. Most urgent items that appear on your 'To Do' List are an indication that someone else has planned their time ineffectively and they now want you to 'drop everything' to help them get back on track. Deal with 'urgent' items only when you have completed your Priority 1 and 2 tasks – if you have any time left over. If you haven't, it will be a good lesson for the other person to get more organized. Obviously, items that indirectly affect your goals – such as utility bills that need to be paid and phone calls that need to be returned – must be fitted in, but you will have plenty of time for your Priority 2 tasks if you work this system appropriately. Either schedule a specific time slot for Priority 2 tasks or pick them off between Priority 1 activities.

What if I have too many Priority 1 items to get through on a daily basis?

This proves that you are:

a. Human

c. Heading somewhere

b. A busy person

d. Working on your goals

However, it also proves that you may need to cut back on the number of goals you are working on simultaneously. Only you will be able to gauge your capacity accurately so be careful not to overload yourself. Practise some of the other skills outlined in this book, such as saying 'No' more often, and you will soon feel in control. The only guide I will give you is that most people find it difficult to truly focus on more than three major goals at any one time. Indeed, Matthew Pinsent has said that he focused on only two goals at university – rowing and his degree. All other activities, such as social events and recreation, were only considered once his daily activities in these two focus areas were complete, and this habit has stayed with him ever since. Currently, Matthew is the owner of three Olympic Gold medals for rowing and is aiming to add to his tally in Greece in 2004 – which suggests to me that this is a strategy that works.

What do I do with tasks that are unfinished at the end of the day?

The first thing to say is that it is not only at the end of the day that you will want to review your task list. You have immediate editing access to your list at any time of the day or night, so why wait to review your list? Reprioritize if necessary, cross off completed tasks and lose tasks that are not aligned with your goals. However, on the issue of incomplete tasks, by far the best thing you can do is spend some time reflecting on the specific tasks:

- Are they really contributing to your goals?
- Do you have to do them next?
- Are you awaiting the outcome of some other events that will affect your timescales?
- Do they still have the same priority?

If your answers mean that some of the incomplete tasks are still contributing to your goals, directly or indirectly, and they need to be completed as soon as possible, move them to the next available date. Other tasks will have to be moved to dates further down the line or even eliminated from your list altogether. As suggested earlier, though, if you find yourself continually moving tasks on to later dates, consider decreasing the number of goals on which you focus. Pretty soon, as you complete more and more of your goals, you will begin to relax about the absence of some of your life goals from your current list – secure in the knowledge that you will get to them at a time when you can give them your full attention.

I have a very real example of prioritization from my own life as I write this section. My three major goals right now are:

- Complete this book.
- Double my contribution to the lives of others through my business interests.
- Build some specific memories with my wife and my little boy Adam.

Now earlier I suggested that three major goals are enough to cope with at any one time, so my other goals have been put on hold until these are done. So, let's look at my current task ('To Do') list:

1 Complete 'prioritisation' topic for book.

1 Prepare for 'work–life balance' meeting with client.

1 Call three potential clients.

1 Pick up brochure for holiday destination.

1 Meet new business associate.

1 Review new website designs.

2 Iron business shirts.

2 Complete tax return.

3 England vs Sweden.

3 Decorate upstairs.

3 Clear back garden.

3 Fix pond pump.

3 Buy new car for business.

I present this list to highlight some of the points I mentioned earlier.

- All of my No. 1 tasks are contributing to my current goals directly.

- All of my No. 2 tasks will indirectly affect my goals.

- All of the No. 3 tasks are important, in one way or another, but they do not contribute to my goals at all. I am sure that clearing the back garden would make life easier right now, but it will also take a significant amount of time – time away from the achievement of my goals. I have not abandoned this task altogether; instead I may choose to employ a gardener for a couple of days.

- Similarly, it would be great to have a newer car to drive around the country, visiting clients. However, I know that I have an 'E-type Time Style' tendency when it comes to major purchases and I like to research the options thoroughly before making a decision. So this task will also take up too much time. It will stay a No. 3 item until either the current car *needs* to be replaced for me to meet my business or family commitments (thereby becoming a No. 1 priority) or I have managed to research the market sufficiently in my spare time to make a good decision.

- I don't think I am going to be able to make the England game (sob!).

Priorities over Time

As I mentioned earlier, the aim over time is to reduce the amount of attention you pay to Priority 3 tasks on your list. Ultimately, you want your Priority 3 tasks to be the most fluid items on your 'To Do' list – delegated off onto someone else's list as soon as possible. This will mean that you will have more time available each day to focus on the activities that are going to move you towards your current set of personal goals. To get good at this, you will need to monitor where you spend your time. Typically, when you start this you will find that you are spending a lot of time completing a load of Priority 3 tasks that frustrate you. Have you ever found yourself saying, 'You know, I have been busy all day and yet I feel I have achieved nothing'? That's probably because you are spending too much time doing all those Priority 3 tasks. Why not start monitoring your tasks today and begin the process of mastering prioritization?

Below is the log of an office-based worker with the following three goals:

1. To complete sales project by the end of the month
2. To improve fitness by 10 per cent within 30 days
3. To complete arrangements for family holiday by the end of the week

Example day	Priority 1	Priority 2	Priority 3
Morning	Sales project plan – 130 mins	Breakfast – 30 mins Commute – 80 mins Phone calls/pay bills – 20 mins Chat with Dave about the local gym facilities – 10 mins Haircut – 50 mins	Chat at coffee machine – 15 mins Personal emails – 35 mins
Afternoon	Sales plan review meeting – 90 mins	Lunch – 10 mins Complete monthly report – 30 mins	Competition entry – 25 mins Sales stats for Tony – 75 mins Chat with Tony – 20 mins
Evening	Internet holiday research – 50 mins	Commute – 80 mins Dinner – 45 mins	Discuss next season's hockey kit sponsors with John – 50 mins TV – 190 mins

Now what we need to do is plot this information on a graph – recording the total time spent on Priorities 1, 2 and 3 – and this is shown in the chart overleaf.

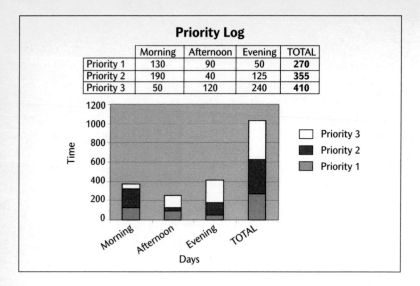

To plot your own chart, calculate time in minutes and record time awake only. Changing your usual sleep patterns should only be an issue when your goals are driving you to do more. However, try not to tip the balance so far that your health begins to deteriorate – you need your sleep.

The next chart illustrates how the time spent on each of your priorities should change over time, with Priority 1 and 2 tasks gradually demanding more of your time than Priority 3 tasks.

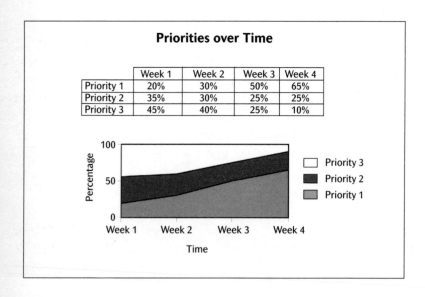

ACTIVITY

For the next 7 days complete the activity log below in order to assess how you are using your time currently. Be honest, especially when considering time with your partner and children. If you are engaged in activities that will contribute to your goals (directly or indirectly) assign them to Priorities 1 and 2; but if all you are doing is breathing in the same space be sure to log it as Priority 3. The key is not to judge yourself at this stage, just to catalogue your current habits and time usage.

Activity Log

Day	Priority 1	Priority 2	Priority 3
Monday			
Tuesday			
Wednesday			
Thursday			
Friday			
Saturday			
Sunday			

Eliminating Priority 3 Tasks

You will probably notice that a lot of time is being absorbed by Priority 3 tasks. The point of the exercise is to help you recognize your personal set of 'time stealers' so that you can put a plan in place to eliminate them. As mentioned earlier, eliminating Priority 3 tasks is essential if you are to start achieving more of the goals from your Life Map.

You will be pleased to hear that there are only three approachs to Priority 3 tasks that you need to remember:

Delegate

Although a particular activity may not relate to one of your own personal goals, it may well contribute to someone else's goals. For example, if you manage a team, there will be people in your team who would look upon some of your Priority 3 tasks as ideal opportunities to develop new skills. Even if there is a small investment of time up front to teach them how to do the task, it will free up a lot of your time in the future.

Employ

Do you remember my personal task list? One of my tasks was to clear the garden. My solution, given that the task was not related to any of my current goals, was to employ a gardener; let me show you why this makes sense. Let's say that you can earn £20 per hour working towards some of your goals and that a gardener charges £10 an hour. The job will take 4 hours for the gardener to complete and 6 hours for you to complete because you are unskilled. The sums work out like this:

Employing a Gardener	Do it Yourself
Pay 4 × £10 = £40	Save £40
Earn 4 × £20 = £80	Lose opportunity to earn 6 × £20 = £120
Result = £40 earned	**Result = £80 lost**

If the goal related task is not an income generating activity, ask yourself how much it is worth to you. For example, if the goal is to spend time with your children helping them develop their minds and grow in character – is it worth more than the £40 you would spend getting the gardening done by someone else?

Ignore

This is the tactic that I know will irritate some of you (for others of you, I know that this will be the easiest option to implement). How can you just ignore that pile of ironing, or that untidy back garden (in my example)? The answer is that you are ignoring only those tasks that are not related to your goals. Many of the chores we need to do are Priority 2 tasks – you may need to iron a pair of trousers for work, you may need to tidy the garden if you plan to spend time there playing with your children. Otherwise, face the fact that you do not have enough time to do everything – consider one of the other two options if it is really bothering you and move on.

If however, you feel *compelled* to do something and none of these options is suitable, admit to yourself that, actually, this task is linked to a goal for you, and then you can give it the focus it deserves in your life without any feelings of resentment.

You need to be honest with yourself about what you want from life, otherwise you will waste a lot of time either doing things that are not helping you achieve your goals or putting things off because you haven't placed a value on the activity. This leads us to one of the biggest time management challenges people face – procrastination.

Overcoming procrastination

❝ Tomorrow is reserved for those who work for it today. ❞

Procrastination is like a computer virus – it creeps up on you and affects all areas of your life. The real problem is that when you procrastinate, you cannot do anything of real value towards *any* of your goals. Instead you 'fill time' and avoid the things that you know you should be doing. To overcome procrastination we need first to understand what it is and secondly to figure out why we let it hold us back. I am sure that we have all experienced times in our lives when we just cannot seem to get started on something that we consider to be very important. After a while the lack of forward movement creates a high level of frustration that can seem to compound the issue further. We look around for some rational reasons (excuses) to support our lack of effort but inwardly we know when we are not doing what we should be doing. Later we will look at some 'easy to implement' methods for making decisions and assessing why no decision is a decision in itself. First, let's make sure we understand what procrastination really is.

Procrastination or Cogitation?

Are you really procrastinating when you don't launch yourself into a new task immediately? Most time management textbooks would have you believe that you are. However, as research progresses into the ways that the brain functions, it is clear that we all need some time to cogitate when faced with a decision or choice. The length of time you need will vary according to your Time Style; T's will need almost no time at all, while E's may take a long time to make up their minds to ensure that they do not miss any potential options or problems. Nevertheless, there is a process that the brain goes through when faced with a new problem that prevents immediate activity sometimes. Let me explain. Have you ever been in a situation where the answer to a question is on the tip of your tongue, but you can't quite get it out? Typically, what happens? Later that day, in the middle of something else altogether, you blurt out the answer (usually when it is of no relevance at all). The reason for this is that the subconscious part of the brain has been working on the problem while you are busy living your conscious life. The same process governs our actions and responses to challenges. Usually, something tells us that immediate action would not be right. If the problem is one that we need to overcome, the answer will arrive, but maybe not straight away. Subconsciously we will set to work on the problem, assessing all the options, weighing up the potential benefits and pitfalls and choosing our best strategy. When we make our decision it is based on all that we know or have been exposed to throughout our lives. In short, it is the best decision we can make.

So, the bottom line is – don't beat yourself up for not making quick decisions. Work to your own timescales, but be honest with yourself. If you are no longer cogitating and are just avoiding the issue, move on to some of the tools for making decisions that follow.

Making Decisions

There are occasions when it is simply not acceptable to cogitate for too long because other people or circumstances demand a more immediate decision from us. At that point what is needed are some decision-making tools to help us stir up our subconscious to work more effectively and quickly.

When making important decisions – in your private life and your work life – you need to be a professional. Professionals make decisions based upon information – and as much of it as they can gather in a *reasonable period of time*. Again, I don't think rules are helpful when it comes to setting parameters on decision-making periods. Each decision will require a different level of thought, ranging from an immediate response up to maybe a couple of days for life-changing decisions.

Here are some tools that may help you make decisions more effectively – actually, I prefer to think of them just as different perspectives that provide some insight into the best decision.

The Goal Map

Your Goal Map is the best decision-making tool you will ever use. As you will remember, each decision that you make can be directly plotted on to your map and you can see for yourself if it is taking you away from your current goals or moving you towards them. However, if you don't feel you have all the information you need to make that assessment, review your Goal Map with your mentor or someone else who can discuss the pertinent points with you. Once you understand the impact the decision will have on your goals, the decision is straightforward:

Contributes directly to your goals	---->	DO IT
Contributes indirectly to your goals	---->	DO IT but review regularly to assess its contribution
Does not contribute to your goals		DON'T DO IT

Pros and cons

This tool is a great way of deciding between two options that are, on the face of it, of equal merit. Obviously, if the decision is between an option that is contributing to your goals and one that is not, the answer is simple, but in this case, we are looking at two options that seem to benefit your goals equally. Let's take a typical work–life balance decision as an example. Your current goals include gaining promotion in work and learning to speak some basic Italian before your summer holiday in Rome. On Sunday night you get a call from the local college to say that someone has dropped out of the Italian course and a space is now available for you to join the class on Tuesday nights, starting this week. You need to decide immediately because there are other people on the waiting list. Tuesday nights are free for you so you say yes. Fantastic! However, on Monday morning your boss approaches you and says that the regional manager is in the area tomorrow and it would be a good idea, given the forthcoming promotion rounds, if you were available for dinner. Not so fantastic.

Don't panic! Just get a blank piece of paper and draw up a table like the one that follows and start thinking about the pros and cons of the two options. Your thought processes might look something like those on p. 90.

Looking at this particular example, your decision would probably be to

Pros and Cons		
	Dinner	**Class**
PROs	• Good for promotion • Good opportunity	• Only six classes • Already accepted • Will make holiday more fun
CONs	• Already committed • Short notice • Should not adversely affect promotion	• Will miss the whole course

thank your boss for the invitation but decline the offer, as you are already busy. Maybe you could even offer to arrange the dinner when the regional manager is next visiting?

This approach does not prescribe a counting approach to the decision (i.e. the option with the most pros or fewest cons wins). Instead, this is just a mechanism for clarifying your thoughts. Soon you will be able to construct this table in your head; however, I would always advocate putting your thoughts in writing as this aids the thinking process dramatically.

Of course, if you had prioritized these options the decision would have been the same because while the Italian class contributes directly to your goal, the dinner invitation is a Priority 2 as it contributes to your goal only indirectly.

You will notice that the illustration uses paper rather than an electronic device; this is because it is easier to see the merits of the options when everything is on one clear sheet of paper. However, similar results could be achieved utilizing a desktop application with a large, clear, usable workspace.

First come, first served

Sometimes even the pros and cons method does not provide the answer and in these cases it is probably best to just go with the first option (which you may have accepted already). If there is so little to choose between the options then it makes sense to leave your current arrangements in place and avoid wasting any more time thinking about it.

No Decision is Still a Decision

Sometimes, it can feel very comfortable to not make a decision about something – but it is important to realize that this is a decision in itself. For example, when considering your financial situation, if you fail to decide which investment option to pursue, you are actually deciding to not invest at all. Your failure to make decisions could be trivial in many cases, but if it becomes a habit, you could start to feel you have lost control and to experience stress, because life goes on whether you make decisions or not. In Chapter 1 we established that this is *your* life, so I would suggest that failing to make decisions is not an option. Take some time to consider the options, allow your subconscious to work on the details, check alignment with your goals, and if necessary, make an arbitrary choice. But always make a decision.

The Results Cyclone

Now that you have acquired some good daily habits, adopted an effective prioritization system and are implementing sound decision-making processes you are ready to experience the power of the Results Cyclone and transform your effectiveness.

Peak performance in an area of your life may well be a goal for some of you. However, in the Results Cyclone 'maximum performance' is about achieving the level of success *you* seek. It is not about achieving someone else's opinion of what a balanced life should look like – it is about achieving *your* balance and *your* goals. As I suggested when we were putting the Life Map together, there is no right or wrong answer when it comes to defining your goals – there is only the right answer for you. Before you take the first steps towards any of your life goals understanding how the Results Cyclone works will give you the confidence that you are doing the right thing. You will expect setbacks and register them for what they really are – learning points. You will expect to work hard to achieve your goals, sometimes with no clear indication that you are doing the right thing. However, you will also expect to win and this is the key differentiator between people who attain their goals and those that don't even write them down in the first place. If you expect to win you will act in a way that is in accordance with that expectation: you will work longer and harder than most people; you will work through problems and issues and you will 'keep your sail up' just in case a favourable wind is in the vicinity (to use a different analogy).

Every great athlete, entrepreneur and entertainer expects to win. Interestingly, though, not all of them expect to win when they take their first steps. Some acquire a greater expectation as the Results Cyclone engulfs them and their confidence, knowledge, motivation and results increase. Whatever goals you have on your Goal Map, why not define the first steps and jump into the Results Cyclone? Whatever the outcome, you will understand the meaning of the following:

❝ Everything comes to those who wait but here's a rule that's slicker – those that go for what they want will get it that much quicker. ❞

Let me walk you through the stages of the Results Cyclone so that you can see, in detail, the ways in which you can utilize its power to transform your first small actions into a life of dynamic results, doubled effectiveness and maximized performance.

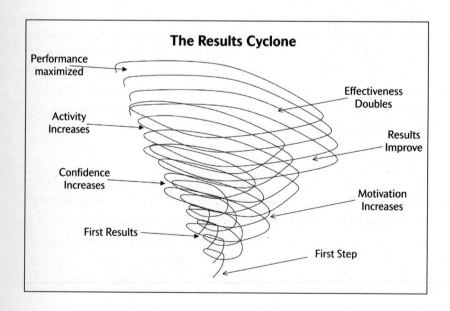

The Results Cyclone

Performance maximized

Effectiveness Doubles

Activity Increases

Results Improve

Confidence Increases

Motivation Increases

First Results

First Step

First Step

For many people, the first step of any activity is often dreaded most – the first day at work or school, the first date, the first calls to promote your new business or the first ride on a new roller coaster. To get over this fear it is important to attack your default mind processes with lots of contrary information. Some ideas to start include:

* Memories of previous 'firsts' that were not as bad as anticipated
* Knowledge of other people who have overcome their fears in similar circumstances
* A focus on the rewards rather than the effort
* An understanding that action cures fear

Often it is very easy to look at successful people and assume that they have always been that way or that something must have happened to make it easy to get started. This is seldom the case; indeed, if anything the opposite is usually true. Just think of the rejection Walt Disney faced before he was able to sell his vision of Disney World, the personal circumstances that Heather Mills overcame to establish her health trust for child amputee war victims, or the corporate giants that Richard Branson has challenged over the years. In each case, their vision of what they could achieve was much greater than their concern about their first steps.

Nerves are necessary and normal. It is important to recognize that the sinking feeling in your stomach is *necessary* if you are to perform well. Most great actors look forward to the butterfly feelings prior to a performance because they know that without them they are likely to forget their lines or miss their cue. The other function of nerves is to keep your adrenalin levels high. This has two beneficial effects: first you have a ready supply of energy for the task in hand; and secondly (this is the great one) you feel fantastic afterwards – *regardless of the results.*

Taking the first step is obviously vital in anything you do, so enlist the help of anyone and everyone to help you get through the fear – even if it means that they need to push you into the path of the Results Cyclone.

First Results

As I mentioned previously, the adrenalin rush that activity creates will make you feel good regardless of the outcome from your endeavour. However, first results are important for a number of reasons:

- They are proof that you are on your way.
- They are the starting point for your performance measurement.
- They have been obtained despite the initial fear and are, therefore, proof that you can do it again.
- They add to your store of examples where you have overcome fear to do something for the first time.
- They provide others with additional confidence that they can overcome their fears.
- If the results are negative, they provide you with a goal to do better.
- If the results are positive, they provide you with the impetus to do more.
- They provide learning opportunities so that you can improve.

For all of these reasons, the first results will push you to the next level up the Cyclone.

Motivation Increases

I like to think of motivation as a motive for action. The definition of 'motivation' in my dictionary refers to 'incentives' a lot, and if you think about it, you now have lots of reasons to continue up the Results Cyclone. We discussed the results from your first step as being either positive or negative when, in fact, they are neither. All results at this stage are neutral because the *net result* is that you have more reasons to move forward than to go back or to stop. The power of these motives will keep you going in the right direction – all you have to do to move even faster is to find even more reasons. Do you know what you want at the top of the Cyclone? Are your goals clear and written down? Have you plotted your route through the Goal Map? Do you know your next steps?

By definition, motivation is a personal thing. No one else can motivate you, although many people will try if you are not self-motivated. Life is a self-fulfilling prophecy – it delivers what you focus on most. Maintain your focus on the things that you want, use them as your driving force and you will accelerate up the Cyclone.

Confidence Increases

Confidence is a dynamic force for action; but what is it that makes people confident? There are probably a number of routes to building confidence, including:

- Knowledge of others' success in the same or similar areas
- Information on *how* the activities ahead can be achieved
- Reinforcement from others
- Positive affirmations (getting yourself 'psyched up')
- Building a compelling personal vision of what success looks like
- Personal experience or achievement in related areas.

However, none of them is as good as actual experience in the specific area that you are tackling. That is why it is only at the fourth level in the Cyclone that confidence is achieved. You have already taken action and obtained some results. You know you can get started and you have also gathered more information on what it takes to succeed in your chosen area. Your newfound confidence is based on personal experience. You have already paid a price and, therefore, you are more likely to go on and succeed than the person who is still struggling to overcome their fear at the first step.

Results Improve

As I don't believe that 'practice makes perfect', let's just say that 'practice makes for improved performance'. Again, I am sure that I am preaching to the converted – after all, doesn't everyone know that the more you practise the better you get? Apparently not. Be aware that at this stage in your progress there will be people who start to make comments that suggest you had certain advantages over 'ordinary' people: that you had a lot of luck; that things have always come easy for you. Well, pretty soon you will be able to prove them right, because if you continue to step out, take action, face your fears, clarify your goals, work on your vision and expand your confidence you will be the sort of person for whom everything seems to come easy.

At about this time, your increased levels of motivation and confidence are thrusting you forward into the arena where your goals can be achieved. As a result of this exposure 'weird' things begin to happen that propel you forward even faster. In sporting circles someone 'on a run' of success with more and more 'breaks' coming their way is often referred to as having 'momentum'. This is definitely a time when 'luck' meets up with 'preparation' and 'hard work'.

Activity Increases

Now that everything is in place and running smoothly you can apply the accelerator to your activities. You have done all the hard work and now it is time to utilize the power of the Cyclone to its full effect. In essence, to change the analogy, it's a bit like surfing. If you sit in the sea and let the waves wash over you, you will get nowhere. But if, as the wave approaches, you start paddling furiously, you will be able to ride that wave all the way in to the shore. That's what happens at this stage of the Cyclone; if you are prepared to increase your efforts even more, you will get even better results. Of course, by now your confidence will be soaring as the results continue to improve and your efforts are handsomely rewarded.

There is also an understanding at this point, based upon personal knowledge, of what your time and effort is worth. You will have been recording your performance from the time of your very first steps and will now have a wealth of data from which you can calculate the value of each activity you undertake. Assuming the value is sufficient, you will work harder when you know the true value of each additional increment of effort.

Effectiveness Doubles

It is important at this level in the Cyclone to remember what it was that got you there in the first place – taking very simple, small steps. Quite often you will see people achieving great success after years of effort, only to throw it away again. Usually, this is because they take their eyes off the fundamentals in favour of approaches that are more complex.

If you avoid this, you can move, instead, into a space that will see you double your effectiveness. This is now possible because not only do you have the knowledge of what works and what does not, you also have the *experience*. You have developed a high level of skill and competence by being open and receptive to change and by being prepared to make mistakes. Most great achievements have resulted from persistence and a refusal to accept one or more isolated instances of failure as being an instruction that it was time to give up. Thankfully, Edison did not give up when his attempts to create electric light failed the first 50 or even the first 100 times. Indeed, this is a prime example of the Cyclone in action. Edison had to take the first fearful step, record the first results, discover some truths, seek some more evidence and build motivation and confidence from a host of results that showed him how electric light could *not* be produced. Only then did he go on to be successful: his hard work and preparation started to pay off and amazing results were achieved.

ACTIVITY

Take a goal that you have achieved in your life and write down how you progressed through the various stages of the Results Cyclone. What were the first steps you took? Were your first results positive or negative? How did you acquire confidence and momentum? How did you know that you were on the right track?

Reviewing a goal you have achieved in this way will add to your list of reinforcing facts when you next face setbacks on your journey towards your goals.

KEY POINTS

➻ The quickest way to become more effective when working on your own is to aquire some daily habits.

➻ Prioritize according to your goals:

Priority 1 = Directly related to your goals

Priority 2 = Indirectly related to your goals

Priority 3 = Not related to your goals at all.

➥ Focus on decision making to overcome procrastination – because no decision is still a decision.

➥ Keep breaking down your goals until the first step is incredibly easy – then take it! Your first step into the Results Cyclone is the most critical.

6 Manage others

Working with others is necessary in all walks of life. If you get good at it, your effectiveness will increase dramatically. Likewise, if you do not develop this skill, your time management will flounder on the rocks of misunderstanding, frustration and shattered expectations.

I start this chapter by looking at three different approaches to change. These are important to understand because the act of people working together will always necessitate change at some level and knowing how your co-workers, partners or friends approach change will save you a lot of time and energy.

Next we consider three truths: first, listening and seeking to listen is the key to communicating with others; second, it is necessary to say 'no' if you want to live; and third, everyone is more interested in himself or herself than you. We'll then have a quick look at your bosses and how you can work more effectively with them and finally review Time Styles to see how they can help you manage others, too.

Change is inevitable, growth is optional

Adapting to change is a skill – anyone can become resilient to change, it really is a matter of choice. However, there are some people who must have been 'hiding behind the door' when the adaptability gene was being given out, but luckily, they are few in number, and most of the time you will be working with reasonable people who will be willing to consider opportunities, discover new paths and absorb different ideas. Nevertheless, it is useful to be able to recognize them and understand their approaches to change so that you can create a useful strategy for progressing your goals without them.

The Way of the Bull

When a bull senses a change in its environment, it responds quickly and dramatically. With scant regard for safety it charges headlong, scattering everything in its path. The human Bull is similarly wired. The Bull's philosophy is 'shoot first and ask questions later'. From a change perspective, the reaction of a Bull is extreme – either embracing it wholeheartedly or fixing on a collision course immediately. Certainly Bulls do not hide their feelings – if something does not fit with the way they want the world to be, you can be sure someone, if not everyone, will know about it.

If a Bull decides to oppose a particular change, you would be wise to let them be. Nothing, not even the threat of severe personal injury, will deter them from their course.

In my estimation, approximately 10 per cent of people charge into this group.

The Way of the Ostrich

Ostriches are funny creatures, generally unassuming and quite happy to go about their business. However, when they sense something has changed in their environment they plunge their heads into the sand and pray that no one will notice they are there. In many respects they are just as stubborn as the Bull, refusing to accept the reality of their situation. Where they differ is in their motivation. Their philosophy is, 'It will never happen around here.' From a change perspective, their reaction is completely passive – letting the changes happen all around them until, inevitably, they are forced to move.

If you see yourself in this category, remember these words I heard recently:

❛ Those who don't create their future have to endure what they are given. ❜

In trying to maintain the status quo, the human Ostrich is opposing Nature itself. Given their determination to oppose such a powerful force – do you really expect to persuade them otherwise?

Again, in my estimation approximately 10 per cent of people hide in this group.

The Way of the Warrior

Eighty per cent of the people you know or are likely to meet are Warriors. The Warrior responds positively to a change in his or her environment, calmly interpreting the impact of the change and assessing how to work with it, using its power to fuel their actions. In martial arts, for example, you are taught to utilize the force of the aggressor, not oppose it. This results in the aggressor looking pretty stupid when done effectively. There's a lesson here for the Bulls – you don't have to fight everything to win the battle.

The Warrior also knows that you must face your enemy if you are to understand him. It is impossible to know everything you need to know if you avoid or ignore the facts. In this way, the Warrior succeeds ahead of the Ostrich – knowledge is the key. All expert Warriors are good scholars as well as fighters.

The key strength of Warriors is that they *expect* change. Warriors have understood that change is one of life's fundamental truths and that they can thrive on it if they are alert to its pervasiveness.

However, before we leave this group, be aware that even Warriors can slip up if they are not careful. The Lazy Warrior can sometimes fall into Ostrich-like behaviour and ignore the forces swirling around them. They may take some coaxing to see reality and rejuvenate their inquisitive minds. For example, I know some Lazy Warriors who, despite having an open-minded approach to many things in their lives, have steadfastly refused to join the digital age and cling to their paper-based time management systems. Despite all the potential benefits (most of which are covered in Chapter 7), they are ignoring the change and some are even taking a perverse pleasure in 'not succumbing' to the 'latest fashion' as they see it. Pretty soon they will catch up, though, as common sense always prevails with the Warriors of society in the end.

The Reckless Warrior, on the other hand, can wander into Bull-like territory, neglecting to make a full assessment of the situation before making a decision. Examples of this behaviour are usually reserved, ironically, for some of life's major decisions – such as getting married or buying a new house. Reckless Warriors can sometimes rush into the decision while emotions are running high and then regret their decisions later. The key distinction between Reckless Warriors and Bulls is that Warriors generally reflect upon their actions and learn from their mistakes, whereas Bulls are likely to look for someone else to blame – assuming they even notice that a mistake has been made.

I draw out these different approaches to change for two reasons:

1. If you are a Bull or an Ostrich (or even leaning towards these extremes) you can identify the key issues, calculate the cost in personal terms and decide to change.

2. If you are a Warrior and you encounter a Bull or an Ostrich on your travels you will not be tempted to waste your time trying to convert them to a more considered way of thinking about change and opportunities. Instead, you will focus on working with the legions of other Warriors waiting for the next change to come their way.

Too often in life we waste time trying to ensure everyone is included. The reality is there are many whom you cannot save and who will not appreciate your attempts to do so – in fact, they will accuse you of being patronizing. Instead, we should be working with those willing to listen, open to new ideas, resilient to change. Your effectiveness with others will improve dramatically if you do just this one thing.

However, there will be times when you come face to face with a Bull or an Ostrich as you pursue your goals so what do you do then?

Dealing with Bulls and Ostriches

I don't want to give the impression that human Bulls and Ostriches are not useful. On the contrary, they are the most useful people to have around when you need to create a sense of stability and security. The champions of change can be a liability when it is time to consolidate all that has changed recently. However, if you do encounter a Bull or an Ostrich on your travels, here are some quick tips on minimizing their impact and maximizing your effectiveness with them.

The Bull

Bulls hate to be ignored; never turn your back on one. Most Bulls, however, are easily flattered. Give them an important role (or at least a title) and preferably one that necessitates that they are responsible for spreading the word about the changes that are occurring. You will have heard that 'none are so zealous as the converted'. Well, by allowing the Bulls to convert themselves you will be harnessing all of that energy positively.

The Ostrich

The key is to go around the Ostrich initially; find someone else to work with or another way of achieving your goals. You need to make it easy for the Ostrich to accept the change that you bring and the best way to do that is to show them that it works without them. Build enough momentum and involve enough other people so that they can join in *unobtrusively*, eventually.

Listen, ask and listen again

As I have said elsewhere in this book, communication is a two-way process – you have to give to receive and you have to listen to receive it well. Listening is a good skill to cultivate and can reap big rewards.

A good friend of mine, a highly paid international management consultant, believes that 99 per cent of his job is about delivering 'common sense' and he is also one of the most effective listeners I know. He has worked in businesses of all sizes and advised executives on issues as diverse as corporate strategy and graduate recruitment. In his initial meetings with these executives he says very little but listens a lot. Quite often the answers to their problems emerge in the conversation, but if they don't, he has learned how to ask some good questions to extract all the information he needs to put his common sense proposal together. We can employ his tactic when talking to the people around us if we want to learn more. The key is to ask questions that focus the talker on solutions not problems. Let me give you an example. Recently, I was working with a team of people trying to piece together a flexible working scheme. Consistently, objections were raised because 'it's never worked like that' or 'the directors would never accept it'. To move forward, we needed to focus on what could be done rather than what was the accepted status quo. I began to ask some better questions:

- If it was possible, how would it work?
- Assuming we could get over that issue, what would be the benefits?
- How could we get around that issue?
- Who would need to be involved to ensure this happened?
- How else could we achieve the same results?
- What would be the best possible outcome?
- Are there other possibilities?
- How can we make this work?'
- Do you know if anyone else has faced this issue?
- Does anyone have any experience of a similar challenge and how it was resolved?

Pretty soon the conversation turned around and we were heading full steam towards some common sense solutions that had been thought impossible only minutes earlier.

Questions like these are helpful for a number of reasons:

1. They keep the conversation moving.
2. They focus on finding a solution.
3. They recognize problems for what they are – hurdles to get over.
4. They move the other person towards a point where the benefits are more real and therefore worth fighting for.
5. They challenge both of you to think.

Transfer that process to your own life now and the conversations you have with your friends and family. How could you ask them better questions when you have a challenge or issue? They will have the answer or, at the very least, they will have a perspective that could shine a different light on the issue and enhance your effectiveness.

Saying 'no'

This is the easiest skill to implement once you understand the benefits of guarding your time. Many people fail at this because they are afraid of upsetting others. What they do not realize is that if they continue to say yes to everything that is requested of them, they are actually creating more problems for themselves and for others. We will look at some specific strategies for dealing with your boss later; let's consider some other people first.

Some people find saying the word 'no' to those who make requests of them extremely difficult. Many clients that we work with fear all sorts of reprisals from their colleagues, clients and even family if they do not comply with their wishes. This fear is usually misplaced. Of course, you want to be helpful and if it is possible to assist those around you without jeopardizing goal-related tasks on your current list, then you should. However, make sure you assess the request carefully. You need to ensure that it is both related to your own goals and that you have the time to do it. Very often, we begin the day with a list of tasks that need to be completed and then we let ad hoc requests get in the way. Do yourself a favour; next time someone asks you to do something – *pause before replying*. Give yourself an opportunity to assess whether this new task or opportunity can be accommodated. If it can, then go ahead. If it cannot, thank them for their invite / considering you / involving you and politely decline. The cost of not doing this is potentially huge – it could mean anything from ignoring existing commitments to double booking and eating into time allocated for special activities.

If you are the type of person who feels guilty about saying 'no', look for other ways of helping the individual making the request. Is it a task that could be delegated to others? Is there someone else who would relish the opportunity? Share the solution – don't own the problem.

2U = 4 Them

The heading for this section is shorthand for 'Not To You but For Them(selves)'. In essence, the point is that everyone is self-motivated and very few people with whom we come into contact are set on a course that is opposed to us as individuals.

Very often, we feel overwhelmed by the demands of others and we criticize them for their behaviour in terms that relate directly to ourselves. For example, we say things like: 'Why do they always do this to me?' or 'What did I do to deserve that?'. The inference from these questions is that the other person is motivated by a desire to make an impact on us directly in some way. The reality is that most people are actually far more concerned with doing things *for themselves*. Once we realize this, it is far easier to overcome feelings of being victimized and gain a sense of freedom to forge our own path.

Your bosses do not sit in their offices plotting your next impossible task; instead they are attempting to work through their own task lists and think who would be best placed to assist them. They are looking to get the job done so that they look good to their bosses. So next time they approach with an 'opportunity', relax and see if your current task list can be expanded.

There are some health benefits of adopting this approach to life too. Life becomes so much less stressful when you begin to accept that you are not the focus of the universe. Road rage becomes a thing of the past, because you understand that the fourth person to 'cut you up' this morning was focused entirely on their world and not yours. Not that this excuses discourteous behaviour, but it makes it easier to smile and imagine all the things that could have caused their bad driving – maybe they desperately need the toilet, perhaps they've just heard that their wife has given birth or it could be they've just had an extremely bad day and need a hug. Just smile and wave them on their way, but don't be offended if they don't even notice you.

WIIFM?

Knowledge of this rule will also help you manage other people. The message is: if you want someone to help you, make sure you present it in terms that will serve his or her interests first. Your staff, your teammates, your colleagues, your friends and your family will all respond better to requests for help if you frame the request in terms that will benefit them. What's In It For Me (WIIFM)? You need to know the answer to this question before you approach someone for help. How can you ensure that this person will feel rewarded for their help? Are they looking for material reward, increased recognition, improved self-worth or are they just incredibly nice and would love to feel that they have helped you in some way? Whatever it is, be sure to phrase your request in their language and in line with their Time Style – not yours.

Managing the boss

Don't Debate . . . Communicate

If you were to ask your boss, your colleagues or the personnel department to name the top three things against which your performance is measured I would guarantee that not one of them would mention telepathy. The same would be true if you looked at the measures your boss works towards. Despite this fact, I hear people every day rehearsing imagined conversations with people, in particular, their boss. I'm sure you will have heard some of these amateur dramatics:

- I just know what he'll say – 'turnover is down, competition is up, there's no room for investment' – so, there's no point even asking.
- She won't believe me anyway, so I may as well take the whole day off.
- I'm sure he's too busy to be bothered by my problems.

This internal debate can only ever lead people down one route – that of misunderstanding and frustration. However, these feelings are not theirs alone – they are also the feelings of their bosses. The biggest complaint we get when coaching managers is that their team members do not communicate enough and they assume too much. Most bosses would welcome the opportunity to get involved and help you work through your issues, but if they do not get to hear about them, they are in a position of weakness when it comes to judging how you have performed. The worst-case scenario arises when a manager is not informed of unexpected challenges faced along the way and is therefore surprised when deadlines or targets are missed. Actually, it is probably not as clear-cut as this. More usually targets are met but the manner in which they are achieved is not as effective as it could have been, resulting in longer-term problems such as stress.

So, the key is to communicate directly as often and as clearly as possible. The following 'Four C's' should help you keep your boss informed and up to date while also giving you an opportunity to find out anything you need to know.

STEP 1 – Check responsiveness

STEP 2 – Clarify questions

STEP 3 – Collect information

STEP 4 – Confirm status

Step 1   Check responsiveness

Don't just launch into the conversation until you have confirmed that the person is listening. Check availability and ask if it is both appropriate and convenient to talk now. If it is not, schedule a time to call back; if it is, state how long you anticipate it will take.

Step 2   Clarify questions

I was once chastized for unveiling bullet points in a presentation one at a time. My intention was to allow the audience time to digest each point separately. However, the individual in question remarked that it insulted his intelligence and annoyed him. I could see how it could have annoyed him (some electronic presentations seem to be designed with that aim in mind!) but it was not obvious to me how this could have insulted him. Eventually, it became clear that by unveiling the points one at a time, I was denying him the opportunity to assess the whole picture and make the necessary mental connections himself. The same is true when you ask people one question at a time. It is almost as if you are saying, 'Depending on your response to the next question, I may or may not trust you with the following questions.' Instead, state your overall purpose and explain the main thrust of your questions. This will aid the conversation in two ways – first, it will provide your boss with sufficient information to be able to answer your questions in a way that is in alignment with your overall purpose, and secondly, it will speed up the process because your boss can prepare and respond more rapidly to anticipated questions.

Step 3   Collect information

This is your opportunity to be quiet. Now I know for some of you that will be quite difficult (especially the I's and M's among you), but having asked your questions it would be foolish to interrupt the other person's responses to those questions. Listen, listen again and, for good measure, listen a third time. The more I learn about effectiveness, the more I understand the real truth in the saying that you have two ears and one mouth and they should be used in that ratio. It would be useful and time efficient to take notes at this point in the discussion, too.

Step 4   Confirm status

Most bosses will have someone looking at their results and asking them questions about status so why don't you help them by always giving a brief statement of progress against targets and anticipated results for the next period. This lets your boss know that you are as concerned about the targets as they are and will confirm your status as a valued team player.

Oh . . . it's the Pointing Finger Again!

Quite often employees have an expectation that if the boss wants to know something, they'll ask. Of course, modern flexible work patterns are making this increasingly difficult as more and more people work from home at least part of the time. However, even in an office environment, the responsibility for ensuring that information is shared between all workers belongs to everyone in the team. If a message does not get to each intended recipient or someone in the team is not aware of the current situation, pause before you point the finger of blame at someone else and remember how many fingers will be pointing back at you.

Communication is a two-way process and just as it is your boss's responsibility to keep track of everything that is going on, you are responsible for making them feel comfortable that everything is under control. Regular status reports at the end of every conversation are just one step in the right direction. You may also consider building in review points to your work or maybe a regular slot in which you can share information.

The benefits of getting this right from a time management perspective are impressive. First, regular slots for status updates will prevent your boss and you interrupting each other to find out information. The home working equivalent is actually worse and is known as 'phone tag'. Your boss phones to see how things are going. You are not answering calls because you need to focus on your work. When you answer your messages your boss is away from their desk and so they then call you upon their return only to find that it's lunchtime and you have a dental appointment. This continues until one of you takes responsibility for setting up a regular appointment to talk.

Saying 'No' to the Boss – Questions are the Answer

Saying 'no' to the boss is the most difficult time management dilemma that most people face. Do you take the job knowing that this will please your boss and get the job off their hands or do you be honest and say that you just do not have the capacity to accept any further work today? Well, the answer in this case is neither. A far superior approach would be to ask some carefully crafted questions.

- I could do that, but I would need your help to reprioritize my existing tasks – which ones would you suggest I reprioritize in favour of this job?
- When would be the absolute latest that this job could be completed?
- Who else could I involve to get this job done on time?
- What parts of this job are vital today and which ones could be postponed until tomorrow?
- How would you go about organizing the tasks on my list so that I could focus on this job?

All of these questions will elicit a positive response from a good manager as they are focused on delivery and collaboration. However, they also indicate to the manager that you have a well-tuned sense of what is achievable and that you are more likely to deliver on time if they help you construct a workable plan. Too often people accept additional tasks without asking good questions because they assume that is what the manager wants to hear. The reality is that the good manager wants to know that the task will be done.

I can only provide strategies that work with reasonable people. If your boss does not respond positively to any of these approaches, you are faced with some more difficult options: arrange a frank and open discussion about workloads with your boss; seek out advice from other senior people in the organization; ask to be transferred into another team; accept it in the short term (but only if you can see the end point clearly); or leave. These choices become easier to make if you have clearly set out your Life Map and you are focused on achieving all of your life goals – not just the job-related ones.

Working with the Time Styles of others

The key to working with others is to communicate effectively. Communication, by definition, is a two-way process. Effective communicators aim first to understand before seeking to be understood, but also know that it is the responsibility of the sender to ensure understanding on behalf of the recipient. Utilizing your knowledge of Time Styles will enhance your daily interactions with others and have a dramatic impact on the amount of time you spend stating, repeating and clarifying information. Indeed, recognizing the Time Styles of those talking to you will help you understand their side of the conversation, while tailoring your communication to engage the specific Time Styles of your colleagues and family will increase your chances of being understood, too.

Many people worry that tailoring their message will mean that they are not being themselves, but this is not true. What you are doing when you tailor your communication is improving the chances of connecting with your co-communicator. The result is less misunderstanding, increased co-operation and minimal frustration, all of which can only be a good thing. The chart below summarizes some of the techniques for improving your communication with others by recognizing their Time Styles. The chart is primarily concerned with conversations of a business nature, but the techniques can be used as a guideline to inform all your conversations. Working from the left, identify your own Time Style, then the Time Style of your co-communicators. Finally, use the suggestions in the 'Communication techniques' column to structure your conversations. So, for example, if your Time Style is T, you will be very focused on achieving results and getting straight to the bottom line. However, if you want to talk about business with your three colleagues you will need to remember the following and tailor your communication accordingly:

I – Smile and check receptivity before talking about business.

M – Smile and have a friendly chat before launching into the key issues.

E – Confirm the topics for discussion and remember to ask for their opinions.

Remember, this is not manipulation – this is *relating*, which means allowing the other person to be themselves rather than feeling that they need to conform to your style.

You	Them	Communication techniques
T	T	• Get to the point • Stress benefits • Agree dates and times • Be prepared with your diary
	I	• Smile • Check receptivity • Suggest fixing times together • Confirm arrangements
	M	• Smile and make casual conversation • Make arrangements together • Check understanding of agreements • Part cheerfully
	E	• Summarize before you start • Ask for suggestions • Specify details • Agree next steps
I	T	• Be brief • Be prepared • Be confident • Stress benefits
	I	• Write down what you want to achieve from the conversation • Refer to it constantly!
	M	• Be friendly • Ask direct questions • Smile • Restate and summarize if appropriate
	E	• Be businesslike • Ask for suggestions • Present options • Agree timescales
M	T	• State purpose first • Minimize stories and chat • Keep to facts and figures • Respect agreed timescales

I		• Compliment them • Set an agenda • Talk in pictures • Write down agreements
	M	• Set an agenda and stick to it • Agree the time available up front • Have somewhere to go afterwards • Set an alarm to remind you to leave on time
	E	• Keep chat to a minimum • Have all the facts with you • Be professional • Remember – a frown is a smile upside down!
E	**T**	• Summarize, summarize, summarize • Talk in terms of benefits • Suggest alternatives • Agree timescales
	I	• Have a joke prepared • Minimize objectives per conversation • Document agreements together • Agree next steps
	M	• Smile • Appreciate them in some way • Smile • Ask them to restate agreements
	E	• Be you • Set a time for breaks • Have the conversations with E's first so that you can concentrate on the more tricky people later.

KEY POINTS

↦ **Getting good at dealing with other people is one of the best ways to improve your personal effectiveness and your time management.**

↦ **The key skills for working with others are listening and asking good questions.**

↦ **Remember, other people do things for themselves and no one is more motivated than you to achieve your goals.**

- The boss wants to know that things will get done, so don't accept everything that lands on your desk automatically – assess if you are the best person to do it right away and seek assistance to reprioritize your existing tasks, if necessary.

- Work to the Time Style strengths of others – it will magnify your own effectiveness and make life a lot more fun.

7 A new approach

What we have discussed so far are the fundamentals of good time management – whatever tools you use. We are now going to move beyond traditional approaches and look at the ways in which the new technology that is available to all of us can dramatically transform your life. Don't panic, though; this will not be a 'technical' discussion. Instead, I want to look at the things that technology can do for us to make the job of managing our time simpler. In this chapter I want to look at the key elements of a sound time management system and demonstrate the specific advantages of a digital approach over the traditional pen and paper systems you may have been using for years. Typically, when I talk to people about moving from the paper approach to a digital platform, they ask good questions like:

- But why bother?
- What's so good about these electronic organizers anyway?
- Have you seen how much they cost?
- Are you trying to tell me that it is better than my trusty old diary that I've had for years?

All are valid questions – especially in the eyes of Ostriches and Bulls. However, things have changed, and electronic organizers allow you to take advantage of a whole host of opportunities that were unavailable previously.

I guess the quickest way to demonstrate the advantages of digital time management over traditional paper-based techniques is to compare the two methods directly using core time management activities as a starting point. All of the tasks in the tables below can be carried out by desktop/laptop applications or handheld organizers; those tasks that can also be accomplished by using a mobile phone are indicated by an 'M' in brackets at the end of the description in the 'Digital' column.

Your diary

Task	Paper	Digital
Find appointments	You know it's in there somewhere!	You type a keyword or name in the search facility and let your digital assistant do the work for you.
Set a reminder alarm	How often does your paper diary beep at you?	You take your pick from minutes, hours and days – how much notice do you need? (M)
Delete appointments	This can be messy. It's only possible if the appointment is in pencil.	This is a simple task that can be accomplished in a number of ways *and*: ✓ the appointment can be retrieved if deleted by mistake. (M)
Move appointments	See 'Delete appointments'. You then write it again in the new slot.	This is easily completed *and*: ✓ you can alter the notes and other information relating to the appointment without needing to start from scratch. (M)
Make appointments	You can write down basic appointment details such as time and place (you may need to write down the time if your paper diary only has units of one hour).	You record basic details *and* you can: ✓ see overlaps with other appointments immediately ✓ add detailed notes for the appointment in the same area ✓ store more than one appointment for the same time (such as dinner and an important phone call). (M)
Review appointments	If the appointment is accompanied by additional notes this may require access to more than one book.	Pertinent information relating to all forthcoming appointments can be accessed immediately and could be aggregated into separate forms if required.

Link with related information	You write in your diary: *Note: See red book for important details.* 'Isn't that the red book you left at home this morning?'	You can link with any other piece of data in your organizer *and*: ✓ access your address book automatically and retrieve phone numbers relating to the appointment.
Schedule repeating activities	How good is your writing hand?	You just tap a button labelled 'Repeat' *and* you can: ✓ specify frequency ✓ specify duration. (M)
Keep an appointment private	How many birthday surprises have been spoilt when a diary has been left open accidentally?	All records can be password protected *and*; ✓ retrieved immediately ✓ shared selectively.

Your address book

Task	Paper	Digital
Use contact details	Where did you file Mrs Smith's number when you ran out of space under 'S'?	As everything is stored in complete alphabetical order this is straightforward *and* you can: ✓ see pages of additional notes if recorded ✓ search for records using other data when you can't remember a surname. (M)
Update contact details	People move so frequently these days your paper system soon runs out of space or runs out of paper which has been worn out through continual erasing.	You can update details easily *and*: ✓ see records re-filed automatically when surnames change. (M)
Add notes to contact details	What was on that piece of paper that just fell out of your address book and down the drain?	Notes are stored easily for instant recall *and*: ✓ they can be copied and moved to other records instantly.

Record contact details	You capture basic details and hope you can read them later.	You capture basic data *and*: ✓ see it automatically stored alphabetically ✓ never run out of room – even the most basic handhelds will store thousands of names. (M)
Categorize contact details	Does that mean I need more than one address book?	You decide in which category to place your contacts *and*: ✓ choose to view your contacts by category ✓ create new categories at will ✓ move people between categories with one simple action.
Keep records private	I suppose you could lock your address book in a safe.	You can password protect individual details or change the security at any time.
Share contact information	Would you like those details photocopied (I'm sorry about the handwriting) or would you like me to read them out over the phone one by one?	Someone needs a number? ✓ Copy and paste and then email it to them ✓ Copy whole address books to disc ✓ 'Beam' the details via your infrared ports – simple. (M)

Your 'To Do'/task list

Task	Paper	Digital
Update completion date	Isn't that what you do when you write out your new list every day?	This is a highly effective use for the new technology *and* you can: ✓ see your list restructure automatically ✓ avoid having to write out the same task every time you need to update your list ✓ create lists of tasks for weeks ahead as and when the information is available.

Categorize	I usually have a couple of different lists that I carry around – the trick is to have the right one with me for the tasks I am doing.	You can allocate each task to a category immediately *and*: ✓ create new categories when required ✓ change the categories of your tasks if necessary ✓ view your tasks by category.
Make a list	Making a basic list is quite simple but what happens when you run out of paper?	You can create an infinite number of tasks if necessary *and*: ✓ tailor your view to show the information you need most.
Add an item to a list	Theoretically, this is simple, but what if the new task is of a higher priority than most of the other items on the list?	You can add as many items as you like *and*: ✓ see them slot into your priority order automatically.
Delete an item	Okay, I admit it can be fun to draw a big line through your tasks as you finish them.	You can delete items simply *and*: ✓ archive them for later retrieval if necessary ✓ undelete a task if you crossed it out by mistake.
Reprioritize	There's no room to slot in this Priority 1 task – I'll have to write another list.	You can change priority simply *and*: ✓ update other details if necessary ✓ add notes if required.
Add notes	How big do you think my pockets are?	You can add notes at will *and*: ✓ recall them when needed ✓ change them at any time.
Share items	Other people can write their own lists.	Sometimes your digitally stored tasks will have a lot of detail attached to them (notes, contact details etc); these are easy to share via: ✓ 'copy and paste' ✓ email ✓ infrared beaming ✓ data transfer.
Receive an 'overdue' alert	Hmm?	How useful is this? *And* you can: ✓ choose how much notice you need ✓ synchronize alerts across several tools to make sure you get the message.
Keep tasks private	I suppose you could write your list in code.	You can retain privacy over any items you choose *and*: ✓ recall immediately when required ✓ share selectively.

Your memo pad

Task	Paper	Digital
Find specific information	I think that point was made by Julia . . . whatshername . . . um . . . at the regional sales meeting last year in . . . um . . . I'll find it, just give me a couple of hours.	You input 'Julia' into the search facility and find the meeting and the important details you need *and*: ✓ find other related data at the touch of a button or stroke of a stylus ✓ link important data as required.
Share memos	Well, I could if I had access to a photocopier.	This is very simple *and*: ✓ the transfer of information can be to as many people as you wish – instantly.
Keep memos private	Do you remember those little notebooks with a padlock on them? Cute.	Some information is confidential – you can keep it that way if you use digital tools *and* you can: ✓ open them easily ✓ share the information selectively.
Review memos	I've got memos going back nearly 5 years (at home in the store cupboard).	I've got memos going back nearly 7 years here in my pocket on my electronic organizer *and*: ✓ a copy on my laptop computer ✓ a copy on my desktop computer ✓ a copy in a secure file on the Web.
Create memos	Ah, allow me to introduce the trusty note book.	Choose your favourite method for taking notes: ✓ type ✓ write using your organizer's character recognition system.
Store memos	Everything is in this book is in chronological order . . . until it is full, then I'll get another book.	This is automatic *and*: ✓ you can move them around if you need them in a different order ✓ they can all be viewed by title instantaneously ✓ you can carry book loads in the same small tool you've been using to do everything else.
Categorize memos	I've got several note books – all in different colours.	You can categorize your memos automatically *and*: ✓ recategorize whenever you need to ✓ review by category.

Delete memos	You can tear a page out of the book, but what about the notes on the back of the page you are tearing?	One tap and it's done! *And* you can: ✓ retrieve if deleted by mistake ✓ delete whole categories if you wish.

Not only but also

And that's just the basics. Chapter 11, 'Advanced digital time-ology', covers some of the things you can do to enhance your time management effectiveness even further.

Go on! Take the plunge. Invest (either money or some time) in a tool that will save you an absolute fortune in your lifetime. Let's say you only achieved some of the benefits listed above, you could easily create an extra 5 hours a week or 250 hours a year – that's more than six 40-hour weeks. Extend that out over 10 years, and you could manage to squeeze an extra year out of yourself (and your staff if they became proficient in managing their time digitally).

If you already own a digital organizer and you are not doing all of the things mentioned because you didn't know they were possible, I would recommend reserving a few hours soon to explore your system or maybe even investing in one of the 'how to' books that have been written to accompany many of these tools. Most look like huge manuals but all can be used to retrieve specific information quickly. Alternatively, why not join an online group focused on getting the most out of these tools?

KEY POINTS

↬ **The advantages of digital approaches to time management go beyond simply automating certain time management practices – they can revolutionize your effectiveness both personally and within a team.**

↬ **The integration of contact data, diary appointments, notes and task lists *in one place* (but copied in several other places if necessary) is a source of stress relief.**

↬ **The tools are useless if you don't invest the time to learn the basics.**

Now that we have assessed what these digital organizers can do to improve your overall effectiveness, let's have a closer look at the specific tools, so that you can decide which ones you will use.

8　New tools of the trade

Before I even begin to tell you about the multitude of options in the digital marketplace I wish to state that by the time you read this, the market will have expanded even further, with new and even more powerful tools. The purpose of this section is to tell you a bit more about the options and some questions you might choose to ask before you decide to invest your hard-earned cash. We will look specifically at handheld devices, desktop applications, mobile phones and some web-based services that are already changing the way people work.

Before you can make the decision as to which electronic organizer you are going to use, it is essential to be able to answer one straightforward question: what are you going to do with it? Once you know the answer to this question, you will be in a better position to choose your weapon.

Whichever route you take, though, even the most basic digital time management system will cope easily with all of the following:

- Contact management
- Storing phone numbers
- Scheduling appointments
- 'To Do' / task lists
- Memos
- Data transfer
- Reading e-books
- Accessing the world clock

- Acting as an alarm clock
- Calculating
- Finding reference sources

. . . and with a little extra investment you will also be able to:

- Create mind maps
- Plan your routes
- Send and receive email
- Create spreadsheets
- Browse the web
- Create and display presentations
- See the latest news and information
- Take photographs
- Listen to music
- Make telephone calls

So, let's take a look at the various options available.

Handheld computers

To Buy or Not To Buy? That is Not the Question

Until about seven years ago I was a reluctant investor in new technology. Like many of my friends I preferred to wait until the technology was completely tested and proven to be of value. Then, and only then, would I decide which model I should buy, and invariably it would be a model that was established rather than new. My thoughts on the matter were completely changed when I attended a seminar given by a very senior (in years) business chief. He waved his handheld organizer in the air and said: 'Life is too short to wait either for the technology to be 100 per cent right or for the price to come down.' He went on to add that owning and using the organizer had revolutionized his life and had broadened his mind to comprehend not only what was possible but also how things could be different and better.

So the question should not be 'Shall I buy?' but 'Which one shall I buy?'

Prices start at less than the cost of an average national train fare and when you think that you will never again need to buy another paper diary or address book – the investment is minuscule.

Let's assume you have decided to invest in your first handheld computer. Where do you start? As I suggested earlier, you need to know what you want to do with your handheld. Is it just as a storage unit for data such as contact details and appointments or are you anticipating integrating your handheld with the latest mobile and Internet-based technology? If you are leaning more to the personal organizer end of the market then I would suggest that you go for something simple with easy-to-use software – in my opinion, the Palm™ platform currently caters best for this kind of user. Their devices are simple to learn, easy to use and incredibly sleek. However, at the really technical end of the market you will find it more difficult to make a choice, as all of the major brands have created models that can cope effortlessly with the list of tasks I mentioned earlier. The key at this end of the market is to ensure that you test the various devices thoroughly before deciding. Here are some questions you may wish to consider

- What is included in the price?
- Is it easy to use?
- Is the display colour or monochrome?
- What is the memory capacity?
- What software is standard?
- Will it integrate with my desktop hardware and software?
- Who is the mobile phone provider?
- What is the cost of key accessories?
- How much does it weigh?
- How long is the battery life?
- What colours are available?
- Is there technical support available?
- What are the dimensions – will it fit easily into my pocket/bag?
- Will it survive being dropped?
- What is the insurance cost?

This is not an exhaustive list but it should help you make the right choice for you.

Desktop applications

For most users of desktop computers the choice is fairly straightforward – you can use Microsoft® Outlook™ or Lotus® Organizer™. These giants of the desktop arena have been slugging it out for years but it looks now, to this casual observer, as if Microsoft is winning. Anyone with a Windows™ based PC will have Microsoft® Outlook™ on there somewhere and, thanks to various corporate deals, Macs are Windows enabled, too.

These computer-based organizers come complete with all the time management necessities – calendar, notebook, address book and task lists. In addition, they offer a quick route in to the Internet, house your favourite links and integrate with your email application. Enhanced versions of the same applications also provide links with standard templates for all sorts of business activities including:

- Business plans
- Invoices
- Accounts ledgers
- Letters
- Sales tracking forms
- Customer relationship management forms
- Strategic plans
- Presentations
- Spreadsheets

However, Microsoft and Lotus do not own the marketplace outright. Your handheld comes with its own desktop software too. In general, these applications are a lot more intuitive initially, because they use the same words to identify the key operations as the handheld. So, for example, the Palm Desktop™ calls its diary facility 'Date Book' which is the same as the name for the handheld diary application.

Nevertheless, recognizing that many people use either Microsoft® Outlook™ or Lotus® Notes™ in work, and that this is where they will be using their handheld most of the time, many manufacturers have provided the means to link their handheld organizers directly with these established desktop applications. The benefits of this are several:

- You can maintain just one diary.
- All of your contacts and other important data are housed in the same place.
- You can integrate with your email seamlessly.
- You don't need to learn how to use a new application.

Importantly, all of these applications are relatively intuitive – or at least they are initially. Scheduling an appointment, adding a contact or creating a task is very simple but if you want to use that information creatively or create links between separate components, it all becomes a lot more complex. You need only look at the number of training courses available to see that mastering the two main desktop applications takes more than just hours of playing and experimenting on your own. As with all computer software, though, new versions are appearing all the time and pretty soon I am sure that all of these tasks will be as easy as falling off a log or pointing and clicking.

Mobile phones

The speed at which the mobile phone industry has grown in recent years has been breathtaking. I saw a film from the 1980s the other day and the private eye was driving through the streets talking on his 'car phone' and I was reminded why they were called that – you needed a car to carry them around! Nowadays, of course, you may not see anything that even looks like a phone when you hear someone talking loudly as they walk down the street – just a wire springing from their ear.

Penetration of the personal organization marketplace has been slow and at best haphazard. No one company stands out for its investment in this area, and even today ventures into the provision of calendar and other time management facilities have been more the result of wishing to provide additional services than a genuine desire to create and support meaningful, useful tools.

This thinking is changing, though, as the mobile companies wake up to the commercial possibilities of providing an organizer on their phones that is completely integrated with their web service. The explosion of text traffic down the mobile networks has signalled the demand for mobile phones to do more than merely provide a sound-transmitting service.

The broadening of the bandwidth for mobile telephony will make larger data transmissions possible but, for now, the telecommunications companies seem to be hedging their bets by providing the support for devices that slot into the newest handhelds.

So what can you do with your phone? You can schedule events, set a reminder/alarm, you can store a list of phone numbers and even create mini folders for your contacts so that one folder contains all of the numbers for one person. You can make notes and share information via an infrared port, and let's not forget that you can also send text messages.

The Text Generation

Now, I know that I am not part of the text generation. I left school when digital watches were all the rage and a ZX Spectrum was the latest in home computing style. Kids these days seem to have their mobile phones welded to their fingers, 'texting' furiously, while older people like me are still struggling to decipher the language of symbols, acronyms and even pictures.

From a time management perspective, though, there are a couple of fundamentals that we can all get right if we are to maximize our effectiveness. First, it makes sense to switch off the incoming message alert when we are otherwise occupied. The immediacy of a text message can make you feel as if you need to respond straight away but, like emails, which we will discuss later, it is probably best to deal with your text messages either when you have a slot scheduled or when you have some time available unexpectedly. It is important to set expectations for the people you communicate with most often. They will soon learn your patterns and engage you in text conversations when they anticipate you are available.

The second fundamental of text messaging is to be clear who you – as the sender of the message – are, especially if you have just acquired a new phone. People will programme your number into their phone so that it can automatically recognize who the message is from, but if it is a new phone or you are an infrequent sender of messages, it can be incredibly frustrating for the recipient if you do not identify yourself.

Apart from these factors, and because text messaging is so limited functionally, there are no other time management issues or, indeed, opportunities with this tool.

Phone/Handheld/Handheld/Phone

The major forces in the marketplace are those of 'integration and convergence'. All of the major technology developers are looking at ways to integrate the various mobile technologies into a device that captures the hearts and minds of the buying public. These devices will reduce the electronic gadgetry you need to carry by 50 per cent and provide more processing and communication power than the first rockets in space.

Here are some new things you will be able to do from your one integrated device as the technologies converge:

- Make video calls.
- Send and receive voicemails.
- Share parts of your diary with friends, family and colleagues.
- Buy goods and services.
- Do remote security checks on your property.
- Retrieve data and messages from home-based devices when travelling.
- Watch television and movies and listen to music on demand.
- Send voice-generated text messages.

Web-based services

All of the solutions we have discussed so far have been focused on you as an individual and how you can get yourself organized. The future of digital time management is much bigger, though, especially as it relates to co-ordinating the activities of whole groups of people.

Work Groups

There are two ways that a group of people can coordinate themselves digitally:

1. Investing in a server of their own and creating their own workspace
2. Employing the services of an application services provider (ASP)

In both cases you will possess a central location for all of the people in your group – whether that be a work team, a social club or a group of independent business people. Typically, you will work through one of the 'big two' application providers – Microsoft® or Lotus® – but this time the facilities are much broader. As well as individual calendars and other time management tools you will also be able to share parts of your diary with other members of the group, create a resource area to which everyone can contribute and schedule events effortlessly with automated invites and acceptances.

An ASP has many distinct advantages over the straightforward Work Group services of either Microsoft® Exchange™ or Lotus® Notes™:

1. It's significantly less expensive. A server can cost many thousand pounds to install and several more to maintain whereas an ASP may charge you an initial set-up fee of a couple of hundred and a monthly rental thereafter.
2. It can be tailored to look like it is part of your service. ASPs provide a shell around which you can construct a service that looks and feels like your other internal systems or, even better, your website.
3. Content is flexible. Some ASPs providing access to Outlook Exchange are also bundling other useful applications, such as Microsoft® Office or other office software products, to reduce your licensing bills.
4. Security is improved. As ASP servers house many groups, security is usually significantly better than anything individual companies could provide.

Office Assistants

The future is even brighter for ASPs when you consider the scope of the services into which they are expanding. Many are building value-added services that will enhance our lives greatly. Principal among these additional facilities is the provision of office services such as administration, business travel and secretarial assistance. Backed by a call centre of qualified professionals, individuals can co-ordinate their work, through the server, from anywhere in the world. Calls can be routed via their 'office' to their location and all of the details can be captured in their diary online and accessible 24 hours a day 7 days a week.

KEY POINTS

- Before investing your time and money in a digital organizer, assess your lifestyle, work habits and time management requirements – then you will identify the right tool for you.

- Handheld organizers are inexpensive, comprehensive time management assistants.

- Desktop applications usually come free with your computer software and provide an excellent starting point for getting organized digitally.

- Mobile phones contain some basic tools but the new integrated technology will blur the lines between mobile phones and handheld organizers.

- Web-based services are revolutionizing the way teams of all shapes and sizes are working and can have a radical impact on the operational costs of your organization.

9 New time management principles

> *Principal Principles are Priceless.*

The great thing about principles is that they just exist. They don't need to argue their case, put on an impressive display or convince anyone of their worth – they are, as the phrase says, priceless. they are also usually timeless, having always had an innate value. Thus, the principles that follow are not new. Instead, I have sifted through the core time management principles to come up with a list that is of most relevance to practitioners like you in the digital world. If you apply these principles, you will integrate time management into your life effortlessly and soon reap the rewards of a life balanced according to your requirements.

In essence, what follows are the 'first principles' of digital time management. As you grow your skills and the technology continues to develop, you will uncover advanced techniques and routines that will enhance your life even more. However, these basic principles will still be important and provide you with a foundation upon which to build.

Just do it!

‘ Today is a Gift, that is why it is called the Present. ’

The biggest advantage of digital time management over traditional paper-based time management approaches is the ability to do things immediately. No need to write anything on pieces of paper, post-it notes or backs of envelopes to take home and insert a new address page in your Lifofax. You can carry your handheld computer with you everywhere and enter information as you receive it.

There are many advantages to having permanent, mobile access to your integrated time management system, but the opportunity to do things immediately is by far the greatest. Force yourself to put information straight into your digital organizer as you receive it, including:

- Appointments
- Names and addresses
- Directions
- Phone numbers
- Email addresses
- Meeting notes
- Birthdays

As I write this book on my computer I have my desktop calendar open and minimized, ready to fill the screen at the click of a button. Throughout the day as I take phone calls, confirm meetings or organize events I put them straight into the calendar. For example, I have just taken a call relating to the work–life balance project we are doing for one of our clients. In the course of the conversation we changed the dates on two of the training sessions, I took the contact details of a manager to whom I need to speak and I took some notes for a meeting next week – all in the same area, all captured as permanent records and all to be loaded automatically onto my handheld organizer next time I synchronize. In the past, I would have needed to write the information on at least three pieces of paper, to erase the training information and to print in the new dates to my diary. Typically, because this would have been cumbersome, I would have copied all the details on to one piece of paper and then transferred them into my paper-based time management system later, creating more work and decreasing my effectiveness further.

However, it gets better. How often do you find yourself in the middle of one thing and you remember something completely unrelated but nevertheless important? This is always happening to me (the product of a busy mind I am told – more likely the result of continually forgetting things in the first place). Most people at this stage would say out loud, 'I must write that down later.' Inevitably you forget later, only to remember when it is too late to be of any use. But when your digital organizer or your computer is always within reach, you can capture that thought immediately. Where you put that information is the subject of the second principle (described below), but if you make it a habit to capture information when you first receive it you will see a significant shift in your effectiveness. One area where I find this particularly useful is in creating items for my 'To Do' list. Very often we know certain activities that we need to do well in advance of the date by which they need to be completed. Being able to add items to my list for several weeks ahead is great for two reasons:

1. I can incorporate the items into my forward planning without needing to think too much.

2. Invariably, these items are ones that I would have forgotten previously so my effectiveness increases automatically.

This technique is especially effective when taking someone's contact details. You may be tempted to write them out on paper first to feel certain that you have captured the details correctly and so that you do not detain the person providing the information. My advice on that one is – don't. Tell the person that you are taking their details electronically so that you won't lose them and won't need to ask for them again. Then, to slow them down while you capture the information, repeat the information back to them as they give it to you. This tactic has three benefits:

1. It indicates to them the speed at which you are capturing their details.

2. It stops them rushing ahead.

3. It prevents you needing to ask for a repeat of the information.

To implement this principle into your life takes some discipline, but can also be a lot of fun. If you feel a little self-conscious when you first try this, make it a fun experience for both you and the person relaying the details. I am continually asking people to slow down while my hands catch up with my brain; and when they remember how slowly that works, they get a good mental image in their heads.

Categorize . . . EVERYTHING!

Principal Principle 2

Categorize, Categorize, Categorize!

Your Virtual Office
• Diary
• Mailbox
• Address Book
• Memo Pad
• To Do list

The habit that will save you more time and be of more benefit than any other is that of creating and using categories. Everything should be categorized, from your digital address book through to your 'To Do' list items and here's why:

• You can keep your digital 'desk' clear.

• Information can be recalled immediately.

• Related information can be filed together.

• Temporary categories can be created to cope with 'events' in your life.

• Emergencies can be dealt with more effectively if you know where to find the necessary information quickly.

• You can impress your friends (and your boss) with your instant recall of facts, dates and critical information.

• Updates can be made instantly.

The Virtual Office

At the very start of this book I mentioned that while everything is changing, some things have stayed the same and in the area of categorisation this is doubly true. In the old days of paper-based time management we were taught to file things away in 'action' piles and work from the top of each pile in turn. The saying used to reinforce this behaviour was:

A place for everything and everything in its place.

Guess what? This principle still holds true. All we have done is to make the task less laborious and a lot more fun. Now, instead of labelling large files and filling them with endless reams of paper in some sort of order (by date/ alphabetically/by person) we can obtain exactly the same results in 1/48 of the time (this is a precise measure, assessed by independent *digital* auditors, and if it takes you longer than this then I suggest you may not be doing it correctly).

So, let's look inside your virtual office and see how we can help you get organized.

The desk

The desk of your computer (handheld, laptop or desktop) should be set up for action. Keep the opening view relatively clean but, most importantly, you should know how to find your most used tools intuitively. Again, I don't wish to be prescriptive and say you should only have icons for the tools you use daily, but think about the way you work and minimize the number of key strokes that it takes to open basic office tools such as your diary, contacts, 'To Do' lists, memos, word processor, spreadsheets and presentation and design applications.

The mailbox

I will say more about email later, but in terms of making the space usable here are some thoughts distilled from years of practice and feedback from others:

- Create folders and sub-folders to cover all areas of your work and life.

- Keep the inbox free of mail by answering all emails that you can immediately and filing reference or answered emails in the appropriate folder.

- Only items that are to be 'actioned' next should remain in your inbox (their presence in your inbox will also serve to remind you to do these items when you next return to your emails).

- Create sub-sub-folders if necessary, to file away mail that it is important to keep.

- Review folders regularly, erasing unwanted folders, deleting unwanted mail, renaming folders if necessary.

When you are finished, your email folders may look like this:

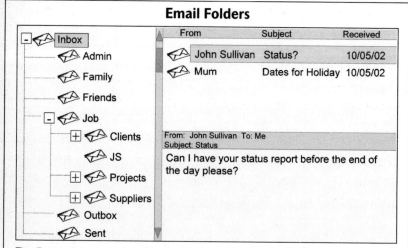

The diagram shows a number of levels of folders on the left ('+' means that there are further sub-folders – maybe one for each project or client). The items in the Inbox on the right are to be done and therefore have not been filed yet.

The address book

Placing contact details into a category means that when you need that information you can recall it instantly and new additions are automatically filed in alphabetical order. Create as many categories of contact information as you need; popular categories include friends, family, administration, emergency, clients, contacts, projects, hotels, restaurants and businesses.

The memo pad

Most paper-based memo pads record information in date order and, usually, information for different parts of your life are mixed together, making it extremely difficult to find later. This is one area where your digital tools excel. Not only can you file the memo using any number of criteria (date/category/ personnel involved) but also you can change the order in which they are stored so that more important information is accessed first when opening the file. Popular memo categories include: meetings, seminars, training, books, personal and projects.

'To Do' list

There are two benefits of categorizing your 'To Do' list items. First, you can record tasks in advance as they come to you and file them in the right place for recall later. Secondly, you can apply focus when working on tasks in different areas of your life because you can restrict your view to show only the tasks appropriate at the time. For example, when completing those necessary chores around the house your 'To Do' list can be set to show only those specific tasks – until they are all done and dusted (literally).

Another good use of categories and 'To Do' list is to create a separate category for each project that you take on. So, for example, I have a 'To Do' category of 'Book' currently so that while I am working on this masterpiece I know exactly what I should be focused on next.

There will be times in your life when you are extremely busy, and it may be useful at these times to use a view of your 'To Do' list that allows you to see 'All' tasks. This allows you to be aware of small tasks that you can complete en route to the next major item on your list and will ensure that your effectiveness is maximized.

Review, review, review

Don't look back in anger

❝ If at first you don't succeed, let's face it, you're not a parrot! ❞

Very few things that we do for the first time come easily. Anything new makes us feel just slightly uncomfortable. Unfortunately, the only way to overcome these feelings is to force yourself to venture out and do the uncomfortable until it becomes not only comfortable but second nature.

Now, if I were to ask you to plan a conference and you had never done it before, you would, no doubt, expect some things not to go smoothly. Well, it's the same with digital time management. Give yourself some slack. Don't expect to estimate everything accurately when you first try to plan out your week. Review your week, learn from your experiences and make 'informed' estimates next time. Continue this process . . .

With a Little Help from my Friends

Another key reason to review your plans is to begin the process of creating your own systems for maximizing your potential; and to do this, you need to capitalize on the strengths of your particular Time Style. I am aware that many books on the subject of time management will try to force you down a route of reviewing your plans at regular intervals; daily, weekly, monthly and so on . . . but what if you're one of those people who frequently gets to work and discovers that you forgot to brush your teeth today?

Again, the technological instruments at our disposal can help us; here are just three suggestions to get you started – try them until this becomes a habit:

1. Set up a repeating note (with an alarm) to remind you to conduct your performance review at intervals that fit with your requirements.

2. Create a repeating task in your diary which stares at you every time you look at your calendar.

3. Set up an automatic email to be sent to you at regular intervals with a template for your review.

I Need a Little Time

Take some time out every now and again to review everything in your life. Complete the Personal Life Balance Questionnaire again and check your Goal Map to make sure you are still on track. Start at the highest levels and then focus in on areas that require more scrutiny. Planning is a skill that can only be acquired through personal experience. However, here are some fundamentals that can make your first attempts more successful:

- Break things down into bite-sized chunks.
- Always put an end date on your activities.
- Make your time estimates high – you do not know all the facts and there will always be unanticipated hurdles to jump.
- Think carefully to assess if there are other people you are depending on to help you achieve your goals – if there are, estimate even higher.

When it comes time to reviewing your progress throw a lot of questions at the list above and see where you can improve or reduce your estimates based upon experience. Ask questions like:

- Were my 'chunks' small enough to manage?
- What can I learn from this about timescales and effort?
- How could I have prepared better or helped the team to prepare?

The final fundamental of reviewing is:

There is always room for improvement.

Back up!

15 Seconds to Comply

Those of you old enough to remember *Robocop* will know that the words above generally preceded complete chaos, destruction and mayhem. The same fear and dread can be evoked when you receive an 'error message' – or, even worse, see a blank screen on your digital assistant – IF you haven't backed up your data recently. Immediately, your mind begins to scramble: 'When did I last back up?'; 'Will there still be a copy of my data somewhere on the computer?'; 'How much information have I lost?'. In general, you feel pretty sick – I know, because it was just such an event that first led me to search for a device that could be backed up. Knowing that all your personal data, addresses, notes and memos have been lost irretrievably is not nice.

So you can imagine how amazed I am whenever I meet people who own a handheld or work with a desktop application and find that not only do they not know how to back up their data but that they have never even investigated the capability. This is the biggest selling point of all modern handhelds – just look at the number of ways you can store your data:

* Synchronize between your handheld and your laptop/desktop application.
* Copy to a removable back-up disc or module.
* Copy and paste specific information between your handheld, your computer software and other software tools such as a word processor.
* Share information with other handhelds via an infrared port.
* Export data from your computer software to other applications such as a spreadsheet.
* Synchronize with a web-based organizer.

Best of all, you can do any of these operations in seconds. Then, if you lose one item (you drop your handheld and it breaks) you can immediately replace it and synchronize the new device with the data on one of the other platforms and you have lost nothing.

KEY POINTS

↦ **Capture everything digitally – first time. It will save you a lot of time and improve your efficiency.**

↦ **Categorize everything so that information can be stored, retrieved and reorganized easily.**

↦ **Review your activities regularly – it is the quickest way to regain control of your life and master your environment.**

↦ **All good digital time management systems include the capacity to back up your data – it is not a coincidence!**

10 Managing life @ digital speed

New communication technology has introduced new challenges from a time management perspective, but there are fresh opportunities too. The key is to remember why the various tools were invented in the first place – to make our lives easier to manage. What follows is a quick review of the essentials and how to get the best from them – email, voicemail, phones and pagers, e-meetings and the Internet. All of these have the capacity to swallow huge chunks of your time if you are not careful so consider this chapter your survival guide.

Email

There is no doubt that email has revolutionized business and personal communications – however, it comes at a price. We have all seen the surveys that show managers receiving hundreds of emails on a weekly basis, but seldom is the real cost of that understood. Reading and writing emails takes time, and for all businesses, including the business of living your own life, time is money.

Rapid Fire

Why not set up some standard responses so that you can just click and send? It is far better to give a response, even a short one, than not to respond at all. Quite often, we can feel overwhelmed by the number of emails we

143

receive, and it can be tempting to ignore emails that we consider to be less important. However, it makes more sense to fire off quick responses to let the senders know you have received their messages and will get back to them with more considered responses soon.

This actually makes even more sense when you consider that you will also avoid being interrupted by phone calls from these people confirming that you have received their email.

Energizer Emails

One of the advantages of corresponding digitally is that you can do so whenever you want. However, this freedom can be difficult to manage if you are not disciplined enough to deal with emails only in short bursts of time. Personally, I find it a welcome break to check my emails at times when I have run out of steam. The change of activity means that I am able to deal with complex messages as well as the fun stuff and I return to my other work feeling energized and ready to go. However, I do know that some people like to tackle emails when they are full of energy so that they can dispense with this largely administrative task quickly. Whenever you decide to do them, set a time limit and stick to it.

Emails are also a good activity when you are faced with a period of 'dead time'. These are times when you would otherwise be unoccupied, for example, when the train gets delayed or someone cancels a meeting at the last minute.

When not actually dealing with emails I would recommend switching off the automatic notification that is included in some email packages. This is an unnecessary distraction and can divert you from focusing fully on other tasks.

Manners Cost Nothing

Think about the recipient's Time Style – how will this alter your phrasing? It's good manners to tone your style, and it also conveys a subliminal message to the other person that you care about them.

Given all the time you will save by employing the techniques above, there will be some time left over to be more courteous when sending emails in future. Courtesy extends beyond just replying to a message – although that is a good start. It takes only seconds more to address the message, phrase it well and sign off. There is no doubt that a communication loses a lot of its power when it is written rather than spoken, and emails, in particular, can seem very abrupt to the reader; with this in mind, it is doubly important to be courteous to deflect any thoughts that your intentions are anything other than to be polite.

'E' Comes Before 'F'

This problem really irritates me. How many times have you received an email entitled 'This is really funny' only to find that you have to scroll down through about twenty forwarded messages to find the witty nugget? So this is the start of my official campaign to get everyone 'Editing' before 'Forwarding' emails. Just strip out all of the information that is not essential and let your friends enjoy the joke and get on with their lives. I know that this takes a few seconds and it is a little bit easier to just press the 'forward' button but just imagine if everyone did this simple task – you know it makes sense.

While we are talking about the various tools available to us don't forget to use the filters in your email package and to categorize information you wish to store.

Voicemail

As with email, acquiring a routine for dealing with voicemail is helpful. A routine will allow you to retain control and it helps others to plan their communication to fit in to your timescales. If your colleagues know that you typically respond to voicemail at lunchtime for example, they are likely to factor this in to their thinking when leaving you a message. They are also less likely to interrupt you before that time to confirm you have the message or restate it face to face.

Some of the other basics of email communication apply too, such as responding immediately to confirm you have received the message and indicating when you will get back to them. Being courteous, remembering the Time Style of the recipient and recording an absence notification message will also reap long-term rewards.

Phones and pagers

Telephone management is a skill in itself – however, there are functions you can use to help you. Let's have a look at some of the best strategies for living life without feeling too constrained by the electronic leash!

It Started with a List

If you want to regain control over your life the best place to start is in the construction of a list. Make a list of the people you need to call today; in fact create a separate 'To Do' item for each person so that once it is done you can cross them off. Writing a list will help you focus on why you need to call and what you need to say; it will also help you avoid making those ad hoc calls that always seem to take a lot longer than expected. Your list should obviously include all of the people to whom you have made a commitment to call. Set yourself a time limit for your calls and be ruthless – when it is finished, move your remaining calls to the next slot in your diary.

Preparation is the Key

The quickest way to get through your calls is to prepare three key points you wish to cover. There are seldom more than three things you will need to discuss and having them in front of you will help you to focus on your reasons for calling.

The second way you can maintain your control over the phones is to prepare them for your day ahead. If you do not wish to be disturbed, make sure that answering machines are primed with a suitable message and that phones that can be diverted are set that way. If you must leave your phone on to accept emergency calls, make sure you screen all other calls.

Pest Control

So what happens if you get a call from that person who just can't seem to take a hint? You know that if you are not careful, you will be on the phone for at least half an hour and you've only got two minutes to spare. Well, there are no guarantees – some people can be quite persistent (as well as immune to subtlety) – but why not try these?

- Set a deadline – tell the person as soon as they say 'Hi' that you only have two minutes; that way they won't be upset when the time is up and you say 'Bye'.

- Ask them: 'How can I help you?' This will help them focus on the purpose of their call straight away (obviously, you wouldn't ask that of a relative or a close friend but for others it is a good way of being courteous and protecting your time).

- Offer to call them back. This has three distinct advantages:

  1. It communicates to them that they are important – you want to focus on them and you are otherwise occupied currently.

  2. You can control the returned call by starting with your deadline.

  3. You can call when you have more time.

What if the pest is you? What if you are the one who can talk for your country? Well done for acknowledging it – now let's think of ways you can help yourself get through all of your calls rather than falling at the first hurdle:

- Set a time limit – tell the other person at the start of the conversation that you have only a couple of minutes and that you will reschedule another time to speak if you do not cover all of the points. You will find that you will usually complete all of the items within the time limit and a return call will not be required.

- Have a goal – put your list of calls in front of you and look forward to crossing them off as you get through your calls.

- Set an alarm to go off after a reasonable amount of time – the sound will alert you that you have been talking for some time and prompt you to focus the conversation on the reason you were calling.

Naturally, you will need to differentiate between business and private calls with these ideas but I hope you have discovered some ways to regain your control.

E-meetings

Conference calls (both audio and video) are a modern strain of the worst form of business virus ever known – the meeting! Luckily, as the cause of the problem is so similar, many of the known cures are still applicable.

Have an Agenda

I apologize for being so basic but this is a no-quibble, absolutely vital, undeniable necessity. I am grateful that I have had to endure only a few meetings that have had no agenda, but the few more than made up for the many – they were disastrous. If for any reason you arrive at a meeting that has no agenda, insist on creating one immediately – otherwise you are communicating that your time has no value and that your diary and tasks (which are determined by your goals) are the property of the host of the meeting.

A good agenda will not only state the topics to be covered but will also have two other important components:

1. An end time

2. No AOB (any other business)

I have no idea where 'any other business' originated, but I do know that it makes no sense. If anyone has any business they wish to discuss, it should be an item on the agenda. Even 'exceptional items' that may have occurred after the agenda was created should be agreed by the chair of the meeting first before being considered by the whole group.

The Time Clock Approach

A couple of years ago I read a story about an American senior executive who had a novel approach to ensuring that people were not late for meetings. He would arrive just before the meeting was scheduled to start and place a clock in the middle of the table in view of everyone at the meeting. Then, if someone was late, he would record exactly how many minutes late and hand them a bill. The bill was calculated as follows:

$$\frac{\text{Number of People at Meeting} \times \text{Average Hourly Rate} \times \text{Number of Minutes Late}}{60}$$

The amount was then deducted from the late person's salary and you can be sure it didn't happen twice.

I thought at the time that this was a harsh way to make a point, but upon reflection I think it illustrates a real recognition of the value of all those who had arrived at the meeting on time. Whatever happens, start your meetings on time with the people who could be bothered to be timely or else expect everyone to be late next time.

What's the Business Case?

There are times when we could all benefit from the attitude of an E-type Time Style approach to new meetings. Before agreeing to a new meeting, or even proposing one, establish a clear business case.

- Why is the meeting necessary?
- How often does it need to occur?
- Are there other vehicles that could be used to achieve the same results?
- Who needs to be there?
- Can delegates attend in place of the appointed members of the meeting?
- What is the projected end date for these meetings?

New Challenges

Teleconferencing has introduced some challenges that need to be considered to ensure that they will not preclude the attainment of effective results:

Unclear communication

It can be difficult to present a clear message on a teleconference call. Both sides of the conversation may believe they are being quite clear but the intent does not always convert into understanding. This is especially true when the participants of a meeting are from different cultures. If possible, spend some time getting to know the other people on the call so that you will gain a measure as to how you will need to tailor your input to the meeting. Check understanding by asking the other person to restate your agreements and even confirm in writing if necessary.

Time issues (in geographically remote teams)

This issue is the easiest to get right but also the easiest to forget when you are in the middle of an intense project. Most digital assistants have a world clock. Set the countries of your colleagues as default and you will always know what time it is for them.

Sharing information

You need to prepare much better for teleconferences than any other type of meeting. All participants need to have received the agenda and any other items for discussion well in advance. If you have access to shared files on a network then this is less of an issue.

Absence of the human dynamic

The biggest challenge for participants in a teleconference is the inability to detect the subtleties of human interaction: the inflections in voice, the use of humour, the seriousness of intent. It can be difficult to get on the same wavelength as the others on the call, and the result is an ineffective meeting. Use whatever tools you have at your disposal to gather intelligence on your fellow participants – what is their Time Style? What are their objectives from the meeting? What is their experience of previous teleconferences? All of this will provide you with some insight as to how you may be able to conduct a successful meeting.

The Internet

The sheer size and scope of the Internet can seem overwhelming from one angle. However, if you flip the coin, you will find that this is an incredible opportunity to save you a lot of time. You may have noticed that I don't talk a lot about 'saving' time, but where the Internet is concerned, there is no better way of explaining the impact that effective use of it will have on your life. The open access format of the Internet can save you many hours, and even days, if you use the search engines properly.

Using Search Engines

Search engines are the most important tools available to us on the Internet. If we use them effectively we can gather knowledge from around the globe in seconds. Just the other day I was struggling to remember who had said 'The reasonable man adapts himself to the world . . .' – one of the quotes in Chapter 3; so, I put the phrase into my favourite search engine and it came back with the answer immediately, saving me more time than I would need to write a whole chapter. Indeed, I am not sure how I would have found that particular quote had it not been for the search engine.

So how do you get the best out of search engines? Well, here are some tips that I find useful.

The basics

Your Internet service provider will probably have a search engine of its own, but if not you may wish to try some of the leading search engines such as Google, AltaVista, Excite, HotBot, Yahoo!, About and Ask Jeeves. To enter a query, just type in a few descriptive words and hit enter or search. Most engines will find results based on every word that you type, so 'blue' would return more possibilities than 'blue lagoon' for example.

Choose your keywords carefully and keep it simple. If you are looking for information on *The Bible*, enter 'The Bible' rather than 'religious books'. Similarly, being very specific will narrow down your results quickly, so 'Aston Martin' gets more relevant results than 'awesome British cars'. Oh, and don't worry about capital letters – most search engines are not case sensitive.

+ and –

Most search engines assume that you want to look for everything you type so the use of 'and' and ' + ' have become largely irrelevant. However, they can be useful for more detailed searches. For example, some search engines will exclude common words, single letters and single digits, but these may be critical to your search. If this is the case, use ' + ' in front of the word you definitely want included or put quotation marks around the whole phrase. A good example would be:

Rambo+3 or 'Rambo(*space*)3'

Sometimes what you're searching for has more than one meaning; 'elvis' can refer to the king of rock 'n' roll or any number of other Elvises in the world. You can exclude words from your search by placing a '-' in front of the term you want to avoid. For example:

elvis(*space*)-presley

(Be sure to put a space before the '-'.)

This particular query would exclude all pages referring to Elvis Presley from your search results.

Or

To search for something that could have alternatives use the word 'OR' in upper case. For example, if you want to find a villa in Spain or Italy type:

villa(*space*)spain(*space*)OR(*space*)italy

Getting specific

Sometimes you start your search with more information or your initial results provide you with some clues and you want to refine your search. For example, you may know that the BBC site has information on jobs available currently but you don't know where to find it, so you type:

jobs(*space*)site:www.bbc.co.uk

Alternatively, you may know an entire phrase. This will return more focused results than specific keywords so to search for that phrase just type the phrase inside quotation marks.

If you don't have enough information to get started, use the categories listed on the search engine's site to begin your search. All the sites have categories such as art, science, politics and entertainment and these provide a simple way to start to refine your search.

For more information on the specific ways that your search engine delivers results, explore their sites. Most have tips and techniques on how to find what you are looking for.

KEY POINTS

- Email and voicemail can be controlled easily if you schedule specific times for them and switch off automatic receipt alarms.

- Preparation is vital for e-meetings – know what needs to be achieved, the Time Style of your fellow participants and set an agenda (without AOB).

- Internet search engines can save you a lot of time and effort as well as doubling your effectiveness when seeking information.

11 Advanced digital time-ology

This chapter could have been entitled: 'Remembering everything and everyone' or 'How to win friends and influence people (made easy)'. The additional benefits of managing your time digitally are endless and still being uncovered daily. However, here are some first (and last) thoughts to get you started.

What a memory!

One of my good friends forgot my birthday recently. Actually, it was a genuine mistake because his new handheld is not completely loaded with all of his information yet. (I was shocked that mine wasn't the first birthday entered, though!) Obviously, this is a light-hearted illustration, but imagine how upset your closest relative or even your partner would be if you forgot their birthday. I know that for some of you this will not be difficult to imagine because you forget more often than you remember and running the gauntlet on missed birthdays has become a way of life. Nevertheless, wouldn't it be good if you could remember every important event and have enough time to buy a card, send a gift or at least call on the right day?

Help is at hand – literally. Next time you forget a birthday, tap in the details, enter 'perpetual repeat' and set an alarm to go off maybe 5 days before the event. Better still, why not do that right now for all of the important events in your life? Nothing could be simpler.

My aim is to be as good at this as another of my friends who never misses any birthdays – ever. She is well known for this and many people call her to check forthcoming dates. Of course, I only have to be good at this once in a lifetime because once the data is entered it will remind me for the rest of my life.

You can use the same technique when entering details of a forthcoming event such as a wedding or a party. If you are attending a dinner party on Saturday night, set an alarm to go off on Friday to remind you to buy some wine. This prompt can then be used to create an item on your 'To Do' list.

Top secret

The following list identifies some reasons why you may need to remember secret information:

- PIN number for credit cards
- House alarm code
- Computer password
- Phone banking password
- Internet shopping passwords
- Bank number and sort code
- Mortgage account security password
- Computer software passwords
- Safe code
- Christmas shopping list
- Birthday gift 'To Do' item
- Surprise party category in task list
- Mobile phone password

According to a recent report, 90 per cent of people use between one and three passwords only to protect everything they own, and these are usually a combination of family birthdays or even their own names. We all know why this is the case, of course – there is no way we will remember a whole host of passwords so it's easier to stick to the trusty 'mother's maiden name'. Well, with a digital assistant you can change all of that because you can now store any number of different passwords and other secret information securely. All of the core time management applications have the facility to store password-protected information that can be unlocked and recalled instantly when required. The only thing you need to do is make sure that you use an easily remembered password to lock these items away or you'll lose the whole lot.

The digital workplace

Digital time management has presented today's organizations with a massive opportunity to co-ordinate diaries, schedule events, collate and disseminate information and build knowledge networks. In summary, teamwork has never been easier to develop. Rather than provide you with a list of the different ways in which digital technology is facilitating work and life I thought I would relate a couple of examples of how people like you are utilizing what is available today.

The Photographer

The photographer responsible for the picture on the back of this book used a digital camera and while he played with the image – to make it look relatively human – he explained how his career had been transformed by digital technology. Apart from the obvious advantages of taking pictures and enhancing them digitally, he had taken the experience one step further to deliver more and provide a better service to his corporate customers. In the past, he travelled to a foreign destination, took romantic pictures of the surroundings and returned home to present his pictures to his clients. They then had to pick a photograph from his selection – even if none of them was quite what they had in mind. Now, he takes the photos and, while he is still in the foreign location, he sends them as an email attachment to his clients. They can then view the photos immediately and within hours he knows whether they are suitable or whether he needs to take more.

The Consultants

As an independent consultant I work with a number of different organizations on an associate basis. Critical to the success of these associate networks is the facility to build relationships and keep each other informed of availability and commitments. One group with whom I work are utilizing the best of available technology in two ways:

1. We each have an account on a shared web-based calendar to outline our availability, allowing the company owners the opportunity to schedule events, co-ordinate activities and fulfil contracts easily.

2. We all have access to a resource database to which we can both contribute and review documents and presentations. This enables several independent consultants to work remotely and provide a service that is equivalent to that provided by much larger organizations.

The Students

I know two students who struggle to make all of their early morning lectures, so they have created a shift system. While one attends the lecture and takes digital notes the other catches up on the sleep she missed the night before (working in a bar to pay her way through college apparently). When her friend returns from the lecture she 'beams' the notes to her and she is up to date. This system has several advantages over paper-based notes and photocopying:

- The writing is legible.
- The notes are usually more succinct since most people do not write quite as fast as they do with a pen.
- The notes can be easily stored and used in other software applications such as a word processor at essay time.
- Notes can be distributed to several people both locally and at distance via email.

The Sales Team

Recently, I coached a team that was struggling to develop a sense of cohesion. As is typical in today's economic climate, none of them held permanent positions and the attrition rate was relatively high with only two members of the team having survived more than two years. As a sales team with aggressive targets to meet they were continually frustrated by the lack of useful information they had about the clients of individuals that left the team. Even simple stuff like phone numbers and directions to the prospects' premises was difficult to obtain; so you can imagine the fun they had when they tried to comprehend the status of the sales process itself.

Independently from my efforts, the team had installed a good sales tracking system, and my time with the team was spent looking at their time management habits and how they could integrate these with their new sales software. All of the key data they needed for each sale could be downloaded from their new system onto their handheld computers and added as a note to a scheduled appointment – along with directions and links to important phone numbers. In addition, they were able to access a shared phone directory that included all the numbers relating to the prospect database.

We also installed some software to allow them to complete form templates with the client directly on to their handhelds. Currently, these forms are emailed back to the office when sales team members next have access to their laptops, but soon they will be acquiring the mobile technology to send the forms straight to the office for authorization while they are still with the client.

Finally, we set up each sales person with an account on a desktop computer calendar so that work could be scheduled and transferred seamlessly. The calendar shows each person's availability and can be interrogated to provide more detailed information on the specific appointments scheduled.

The Business Meeting

If you have ever attended a general business meeting that is open to people from many businesses, you will know that, invariably, you go home with a stack of business cards that have been thrust into your hand at every available opportunity. When you get home you then have a separate task of copying all of those details into your contacts book and this can take several hours. In meetings where all the attendees have handheld computers the process can be completed in a matter of minutes. In that time, everyone can 'beam' their digital business card to everyone else in the room and receive everyone else's cards in return. As long as the infrared ports are compatible this is a straightforward exercise and can be much more effective than standard business card swapping because you have an opportunity to add a whole host of notes to your 'card' for the recipient to read later.

Expansion – a questioning approach

Most handhelds and desktop applications can be expanded to incorporate all kinds of accessories and peripherals that are designed to do everything faster, better and smarter. However, this is the point where I pass on a general health warning – make sure that any new technology you acquire is really going to provide you with additional benefits – as you have read, the array of things you can do already with the standard tools is impressive, and some accessories and additional software can slow down the performance of your time management assistant, reducing your overall effectiveness. So be selective.

Here are just some of the things that can be added to handhelds. Some of these are standard with some models, but most are available as accessories or as add-ons:

- An MP3 player
- A modem
- A camera
- A phone
- Games

- E-books
- Reference manuals
- Advanced computer software
- A keyboard
- A voice recorder

In the meantime, you should keep your eyes and ears open. As the technology continues to converge and integrate, even simple tools will become available at more affordable rates. Who knows even the most stubborn Bull or unyielding Ostrich may join us in the twenty-first century!

KEY POINTS

➴ The memory capacity of digital assistants is awesome and can help even the most forgetful person become a thoughtful and caring individual!

- Storing secret information has never been easier or more secure.
- New technology is facilitating more effective ways of working that are available to everyone, not just the big corporations.

Close – a digital world of opportunity

So now it's over to you. If you have not done any of the initial exercises why don't you go back now to Chapter 2? Start by piecing your Life Map together and go on to identify your first set of goals. Then you'll be able to break them down, isolate the first small step and jump into the Results Cyclone – it really is as simple as that! To finish, I thought I would provide you with one last example of someone who is using their time effectively to live an extraordinary life and then make a request to you to share your story.

The digital entrepreneur

Twenty-four-hour opportunity awaits the digital entrepreneur. The Internet never sleeps, so why should you? Perhaps you could work all night when there are less leisure and family activities to pursue. Sleep patterns may well change as individuals learn how to 'power-nap' their way to fame and fortune.

A Change is as Good as a Rest

A good friend of mine recoiled in horror when she read the title of this book. 'Does this mean that there won't be any time for rest and recreation?' she asked. 'Absolutely,' I said. Sensing that this was not the answer she was looking for, I added, 'Unless you get your life under control.' You see, the opportunity for companies to work around the clock, tuning in to the global markets as and when they open for business, will not be lost on the more enterprising business owners out there, keen to forge ahead while they can and capture bigger and bigger markets whilst their competitors are decrying the '9 to 5 straightjacket' that constrains their business. This, in turn, will mean more 'opportunities' for employees to work around the clock, too. If you work in the following areas, I can imagine a time pretty soon when your boss is going to be discussing some strange shift patterns with you:

- Business services
  - Administration
  - Secretarial
  - Finance
  - Marketing
  - Advertising
  - Public Relations
  - Publishing
- Education
  - Further education establishments
  - Corporate training
- Retailing
  - High street shops
  - Takeaways
- Service industry
  - Financial services
  - Restaurants
  - Entertainment
- Customer Service
  - Call centres
  - Information hubs
  - Reference services

Logically, there is no reason why all of these industries are not organized this way now. Your customers are waiting for you. In the UK, the growth of 24-hour supermarkets and the number of customers at roadside garages at 10:00 p.m. is pointing the way. Changing work patterns, 24-hour manufacturing processes and the general lack of work–life balance is creating a demand for increased service at times when most of the business world is asleep. But in the short term, digital entrepreneurs will have to look elsewhere for the 24-hour opportunities they seek.

I'd like you to meet David Larson. I last met him when I was writing about the 'Millennium Worker' in the 'Nil By Mouth' report produced for Investors In People and Accenture. The name is fictitious, but the rest is factual and based on his current activities.

I relate this information about my friend for two reasons:

1. To help you understand that getting good at managing your time, focusing on your dream and organizing your life can reap the rewards you are seeking

2. To provoke some 'possibility thinking' – what could you achieve in the next year if you organized your time more flexibly?

This is a typical day for David:

07:30   David arrives at his office in London.

   David Larson owns a company that provides accountancy services to its clients through the use of a bank of associates. Each associate is self-employed and is therefore not an overhead to the business when they are not busy. There are only two support staff in place to field enquiries and to deal with basic administrative tasks.

   His first job is to check the 'snail mail' for anything important, then he settles down for the first meeting of the day.

08:00   Teleconference with his three partners in Berlin, Melbourne and San Francisco.

   David established the model for his business and then sourced his partners through the Internet. Each has a stake in the business and can drive the business as hard as they care given the flexibility of the company's structure. They usually 'meet' at this time as it fits in with the personal lives of all four of them.

09:30   Conversation with the Office Assistant to clarify forthcoming work-loads and book in new work.

The Office Assistant is an Internet based service that provides small business owners with the host of services that would normally be whole departments in big business. Secretarial, courier and training services can all be arranged through a call centre and through the Web.

Happy that everything is in order, David leaves for the day.

10:00   Game of tennis at the local sports centre with his coach.

David varies the activities he does at this time to ensure a thorough cardiovascular routine throughout the week.

12:00   Lunch with wife.

13:00   Bed.

15:30   Sits at his desk and begins the process of researching some potential sponsors for the children's charity he established a couple of months ago.

He is currently looking for local business people to help fund the creation of a day centre for underprivileged kids.

David quickly prepares a shortlist of potential investors and begins the process of setting up meetings with as many as possible.

17:00   Family time – the kids are home from school and it's time to play.

20:00   David arrives at the house of a business associate in his web-based referral marketing business to review the plan for the month ahead.

22:00   Joins an online live discussion forum hosted in the USA.

This space in his diary is usually reserved for skills building and training, but today's discussion is about one of his businesses – e-book publishing.

24:00   David stays in his office and has several conversations with his New York colleagues about the new authors they will be promoting on their e-book website.

David was introduced to the world of e-books a couple of years ago and thought it was an ideal way to get unpublished authors into the public arena. Since then, his company has helped 500 people get started. From a business perspective, David acts as a reseller for their work and takes a commission accordingly.

02:00   Bed again.

Total hours worked = 8.5 hours

Charity work = 1.5 hours

Family time = 4 hours

Sleep = 8 hours

Fitness = 2 hours

David Larson started on this unusual journey 5 years ago when most people were just starting to realize that it might be a good idea to get an email address. His dream is to be financially independent in 3 more years (before he gets to 40) so that he can retire and play golf. His current net worth is approaching £1 million, but he has calculated that he needs about five times this amount if he is to pay for his children's education and fully establish his children's charity.

The key for David is to create a work–life balance that works for him and his family. Prior to changing his work routines, David worked for one of the major accounting companies in the City, working 14 hours a day, travelling for two hours and seeing his wife for a couple of hours (his children were already asleep). Now he has more time available to spend with his family and, through utilizing some of the technology available for his business activities, he also has time available to do some of the charity work he always dreamed of doing.

You Unlimited

Work–life balance is only a small decision away. Equally, there are unlimited opportunities for you to pursue if you will only believe in your dreams.

The communication technology advances that have occurred in recent years have made it even more possible to fuel your entrepreneurial fire. International businesses can be created overnight, global teams 'formed, stormed and normed' in weeks and empires built in months and years.

If technology is not your thing, maybe you could think about providing a specific service to the millions of people all around you that are struggling to 'get everything done' as the work pressures continue to mount? Or perhaps you could do something in the entertainment arena, the fastest growing industry in the world?

Whatever you choose to do, effective time management will be your tool for unlimited success:

❝ The good news is that your future is in your hands,

The bad news is that your future is in your hands. ❞

The time master

Are you a 'time master'? Has this book inspired you to change some things in your life and enabled you to double your effectiveness? If so, why not write your story? Capture what works for you, what else you have used to maximize your effectiveness and balance your life. I'm looking forward to hearing your stories so please, feel free to write to me and who knows, we may even write a follow-up to help a few more people just like you.

Have a wonderful life!

Appendix I Personal Life Balance Questionnaire

See questionnaire pages 170–171.

Personal Life Balance Questionnaire

Answer all questions by writing the appropriate number in the box provided, using the following scale:

Rarely or never true = 1 Some of the time = 2 Most of the time = 3 All of the time = 4

	Rarely or never true (1)	Some of the time (2)	Most of the time (3)	All of the time (4)
1 My inboxes are clear (email / voicemail / paper)	☐	☐	☐	☐
2 I am in control of the information I need	☐	☐	☐	☐
3 I spend quality time with my family	☐	☐	☐	☐
4 I make time for hobbies and interests	☐	☐	☐	☐
5 I follow a regular exercise plan	☐	☐	☐	☐
6 I spend 'quiet' time with my partner	☐	☐	☐	☐
7 I plan my television viewing	☐	☐	☐	☐
8 I get enough sleep	☐	☐	☐	☐
9 I make time to read	☐	☐	☐	☐
10 I am up to date with what is happening in the world	☐	☐	☐	☐
11 I read quality books to learn new things	☐	☐	☐	☐
12 I make time for fun	☐	☐	☐	☐
13 I never say 'I haven't got time'	☐	☐	☐	☐
14 I make time to spend with friends	☐	☐	☐	☐
15 I pay bills on time	☐	☐	☐	☐

16 I take regular holidays

17 I remember important events

18 I remember birthdays and anniversaries

19 I never lose important information

20 I am organized

21 I am focused

22 Personal development is key to me

23 I watch educational / informational programmes

24 I attend seminars and other learning events

25 I am always on time

26 I like to prioritize events and activities

27 I have high energy levels

28 I have my goals written down

29 I find it easy to say 'No'

30 I am working on my life goals

TOTALS

Calculate your overall score by adding together the totals of the four columns.

My Personal Life Balance score is :

Personal life balance questionnaire – implications

Life Areas

Add up your scores for the four key life areas below. Then use the formula to determine your effectiveness in each area:

Live (questions 4, 5, 7, 8, 12, 16, 26, 27, 28, 29, 30)

Formula: your score / 44 × 100 ☐%

Love (questions 3, 6, 13, 14, 18)

Formula: your score / 20 × 100 ☐%

Learn (questions 9, 10, 11, 22, 23, 24)

Formula: your score / 24 × 100 ☐%

Leave A Legacy (questions 1, 2, 15, 17, 19, 20, 21, 25)

Formula: your score / 32 × 100 ☐%

Appendix II Recommended reading

The following selection of books has helped me, in different ways, to focus on the key areas of my life – I hope you enjoy them.

Beavis, Wes, *Dating The Dream*, The Catalyst Group, 1996

Brown, Les, *Live Your Dreams*, Avon Books, 1994

Carnegie, Dale, *How to Win Friends and Influence People*, Hutchinson, 1994

Gorman, Mark, *Getting a Message to Garcia* (Audio Book)

Haley, Alex, *Roots*, Dell Publishing, 1976

Hopkins, Tom, *The Official Guide to Success*, HarperCollins Publishers, 1994

Mandino, Og, *The Spellbinder's Gift*, Ballantine Books, 1995

Maxwell, John C, *Failing Forward*, Thomas Nelson Publishers, 2000

Parsons, Rob, *The Heart of Success – Making it in business without losing in life*, Hodder & Stoughton, 2002

Robbins, Anthony, *Notes From A Friend*, Simon & Schuster Ltd, 1996

Rohm, Dr Robert, *Positive Personality Profiles*, Personality Insights Inc., First Edition, 1992

Rohn, Jim, *7 Strategies for Wealth and Happiness*, Primapublishing, 1996

Schwartz, David J, PhD, *The Magic of Thinking Big*, Simon & Schuster Ltd, 1995

Turner, Colin, *Swimming with Piranhas makes you Hungry*, InToto Books, 1998

To follow up on any of the information in this book,
or for specific information on:
Seminars
Coaching
Corporate Speaking
Workshops

please contact: **SIMON PHILLIPS**

Liberty Suite, 261 Dedworth Road, Windsor, SL4 4JS
Tel: (+44) 1753 623793
email: simes@simonphillips.biz
or visit us at www.simonphillips.biz

For information on our other services such as:
Digital Time Management Training Course
In-House Training
Work–Life Balance
Virtual Teams
Managing Change

please contact: **SIMESCO LIMITED**

at www.simesco.co.uk or email: info@simesco.co.uk

Index